Dedication

This book is dedicated to everyone, young benefits that fishing can provide our local communities and what it can do for our wellbeing.

Independently published

1st edition 20th March 2023

2nd Edition 5th July 2023

Written Text © Ben Harragan 2023

Photography © Ben Harragan 2023

Photography in 'Fish facts' section © HHDAS committee 2023

Illustrations © Ben Harragan 2023

Let's Go Fishing! logo and design format © Ben Harragan 2023

All product branding in the images used within this handbook are copyright of their respective owners, we may own the products, but we do not own the rights to any branding or any patents. These images are for illustration purposes only and serve only in an educational capacity.

All rights reserved, including the right to reproduce this book or portions thereof in any form or any means, electronic or mechanical, including photocopying, recording, or by any information storage retrieval system, without permission from the copyright owner.

The author asserts the moral right to be identified with this work.

ANGLING & MENTAL HEALTH INITIATIVE

The Angler's Handbook

Volume I

A comprehensive guide

CONTENTS

Angling Essentials	3
Mental Health Benefits	9
Fishing Basics – Part 1	16
Fishing Basics – Part 2	52
Fish Facts	79
Bait Basics	87
UK Fish Species	115
Knot Knowledge	175
Float Fishing	189
Feeder Fishing	209
Ledger Fishing	214
Essential Links	219

Angling Essentials

A beginner's guide to fishing

What is fishing?

Fishing, which is also known as angling, is the sport of catching fish. A person who goes fishing is known as an angler or a fisherman/woman. Fishing can be either freshwater or saltwater, typically using a rod, line, and a hook. Fishing originated as a means of providing food for survival. In its most basic form, fishing is throwing out a fishing line and pulling in the fish when it goes for your baited hook or fishing lure.

Throughout the history of fishing, various fishing disciplines have emerged that target specific fishing conditions and species of fish. These variations have their own unique fishing equipment, know how, and technical skills. These may be specific to the type of water in which an angler will be fishing, or the kind of fish targeted. There are three main types of fishing: Coarse, Game and Sea.

Coarse fishing is specific for any species of fish in freshwater except game fish. This can either be in a lake, pond, river, or stream.

Game fishing pertains to the pursuit of Trout, Sea Trout and Salmon.

Sea fishing, as its name suggests, is fishing for species that inhabit the sea.

An offshoot of coarse angling, or a sub-genre, is specimen fishing. Specimen anglers target the bigger, prime species of freshwater fish, most popular is the Carp (Carp is the common name for fish belonging to the family Cyprinidae - *see the UK fish species section*). These fish can grow to very big weights (up to 68lb in 2016) and since the 1950's, anglers have specifically targeted these specimen fish. Specimen anglers also fish specifically for Barbel, Tench, and the bigger sized fish of other species. Targeting predatory fish such as Pike, Perch, and Zander, is also very popular more so in the colder months.

What is a Rod Licence?

Any angler (aged 12 years or over) fishing in England (except the Tweed), Wales or the Border Esk and its tributaries in Scotland, must have an Environment Agency rod licence. This covers fishing for salmon, trout, freshwater fish, and eel dependant on what license you purchase (there are game fishing licenses as well as coarse and there is one for both)

You can buy your licence at Post Offices, by telephone or online. It is an offence to fish for freshwater fish and eels without a valid rod licence and if you do you may be liable for a fine of up to £2,500. If you are serious about taking up fishing, then it is cheaper to buy a 12-month licence. If you are unsure, then daily, and weekly licences are available.

What is the Close Season?

Close season means no fishing (you are not allowed to fish in certain areas in a specified period). The close season is a period that allows the fish to spawn and reproduce uninterrupted by the pressures that fishing can bring during this time. Many species spawn during this period, some of which migrate into the river systems from the sea. If you are fishing lakes or venues which are open during the close seasons, be aware of fish spawning during this time, usually most species come close to the bank and chase each other. They normally do this in small groups, so you will notice they are less concerned with your presence, and it is best to leave them to their business.

UK Coarse fish - Close season 15th March to 15th June (inclusive)

The coarse fish close season applies to all rivers, streams, and drains in England & Wales. This does not apply to most still waters, however, there are some exceptions that retain the close season. Recent byelaw changes mean that the coarse fish close season does not apply to most canals in England and Wales, although there are some exceptions (please check with your local authority). In areas where the close season is not applicable, fishery owners and angling clubs are free to introduce a close season if they wish to.

What are the risks?

Much the same as having a walk out into a woodland area, or aside a riverbank, be aware of the possible dangers around you. These could include things like steep banks, unstable edges, slippery surfaces, and other trip hazards such as tree roots. The water itself is a hazard, the most obvious is a potential to drown, but also there can be under water hazards that you will not know about as well as water born viruses or diseases.

Always wear appropriate clothing for the weather, check local weather forecasts whenever possible. Fishing under trees can be unsafe in windy conditions. Be aware of falling branches and report any damaged trees to your venue if possible. Remember to keep covered or wear sunscreen when the sun is out, or UV factors are high (Check weather reports for this). Too much exposure to sun can cause skin cancers. It is always best to wear good non-slip footwear at all times, wellies are ok, but a good general-purpose boot would be advantageous. Always carry a torch / head torch (and a spare) in case you have to pack up in the dark or when going night fishing. Carry a mobile phone for emergency purposes, as well as a basic first aid kit (this can be left in the car or carry a small lightweight kit).

Other risk factors are the kit you use, such as hooks, line, and scissors etc. Hooks pose one of the worse risks, this can be on a float rig or on a lure, either way, at any point you get a hook in your body, you will need to go to hospital, do not attempt to remove it yourself, especially if it is barbed!

Important Safety Tip! Always take your litter home! This includes food wrappers, discarded line or other forms of litter. It can pose a serious risk to the environment and wildlife.

WARNING! **Never fish in any type of electrical storm, most fishing rods/poles are made of carbon, you will be at high risk of an electrical shock.**

IMPORTANT SAFETY ADVICE

Weil's Disease

Weil's disease (Leptospirosis) is a bacterial infection carried by rat's urine which contaminates water and the banks of rivers and ponds. There are a number of simple precautions you can take against Weil's disease and other bacterial infections:

- Clean and disinfect any wounds that occur at the waterside.
- Wash your hands.
- Do not put your hands in your mouth after immersing in water and never place bait or fishing line in your mouth.
- Do not touch dead animals, especially rats.
- If you develop flu like symptoms that persist, tell your doctor that you may have been exposed to leptospirosis so that they can consider it in the diagnosis.

For more information on the disease, symptoms or more on how to get help, please visit their website.

https://www.nhs.uk/conditions/leptospirosis/

or use the QR code below.

Mental Health Benefits

A look at how fishing can be good for wellbeing

How can fishing help with wellbeing?

Fishing is first and foremost a sport, enjoyed by millions of people worldwide. But it can also bring other benefits, such as being in a relaxed and calming environment or learning new skills to catch your first fish. Fishing can aid in reducing depression, relieving stress and anxiety. Every fishing venue will be abundant with wildlife, from the humble Water Boatman to the red chested Robin and surrounding yourself with nature and wonder can boost your mental health. Learning how to relax and de-stress from the modern world as well as enjoying the benefits from the plant life are just a few of the positive effects of fishing.

What benefits can fishing have?

When you go fishing, it requires focus and awareness, and this can take your mind of life stresses or any internal conflicts. Some of the positive effects of fishing are very similar to meditation. The main resulting factor of this may help you to reduce any anxieties you are currently experiencing, can help fight off depression, and will help to promote relaxation.

Recent studies have shown that fishing lowers your stress levels (known as cortisol levels), and those that fish regularly have experienced positive effects that can last for as long as two to three weeks after.

Going fishing has even been used to help people who have experienced considerable trauma or suffer from PTSD.

Being around moving water has been proven to make people feel calmer and more creative. It is also known that water triggers our parasympathetic nervous system. This helps to lower heart rate, lower blood pressure, your digestion is stimulated, and your body can relax. Researchers also found that listening to natural sounds can invoke a more relaxed physical state. This indicates the body is moving away from a "fight or flight" response to a peaceful one. It provides soothing sensory experiences.

The sound, smell, and sight of water can be very soothing. It also benefits the mind and soul bringing a calm, positive state of mind.

Fishing is never the same with each trip you take, one day you catch fish on a certain bait, the next day it can be ineffective. One trip the fish will be in a certain spot, the next time they may not be, so adapting the way we fish helps us to learn how to overcome small obstacles. Learning to change the type of bait you use, finding that new fishing spot, or working out that new rig may seem challenging. However, all these challenges are helping you to develop problem solving skills, improving your cognitive functions and can improve creative thinking.

Fishing can also teach an angler patience, more so with the children. As children learn to wait for a bite, they learn patience. They learn how to stay calm when they lose a fish, experience ways on how to adapt and change to get those fish. Even just being outside has been proven to reduce symptoms of ADHD.

Fishing tends to take a lot of dexterity as some fishing lines are very thin and easily tangled, this needs good hand eye coordination as well as nimble fingers. Attaching bait to hooks takes special care, and a successful cast depends on some precise timing and practice. These small tasks help develop the fine-motor skills. Learning something new is also very good for building cognitive functions. In a world filled with digital devices and things like the internet, kids and adults alike are constantly exposed to it and can often be consumed by them. Getting out and going fishing gets everyone off their digital devices and promotes an appreciation for the natural environment.

Anglers also get the chance to experience the adventure side of fishing, like wading through streams or walking through woodlands that are filled with wildlife.

There are also the physical aspects that fishing brings, with the main aspect being walking. The walk to your venue with your tackle or walking up and down a river to spot the fish provides a good cardiovascular workout. There is also the low-impact exercise of fishing to consider, like casting or playing fish. This engages your shoulders, back, core, arms, and legs, improving your balance and working your muscles. The other aspects and benefits of fishing are having the chance to soak up the sun. Vitamin D from the sun improves your immune system and promotes cell growth, helping to fight off illness and disease. It is also a very good mood enhancer. All of this can have a positive impact on mental health, good wellbeing, with a peaceful and relaxed mind. Whether you are affected by mental health issues or not, it can only benefit people to participate in something so positive to our souls. You can also meet new people, learn new things, and experience something unique, there is always something for everyone to gain from fishing.

The Angling Trust have been playing a pivotal role in the mental health movement and its link to fishing, with their 'Get Fishing' scheme. This allows participants to experience fishing for free, without the investment in rods, reels, and tackle. The Get Fishing for Wellbeing project is for everyone who might benefit from involving recreational fishing in the way that they manage conditions that benefit from a "Social Prescribing" approach to healthcare. For more information on these experiences, please visit their website.

https://anglingtrust.net/getfishing/getfishingforwellbeing/

Besides fishing, there are quite a few things we can do to add to our 'toolbox' of life and good wellbeing. For more information on mental health please visit the mental health UK website.

https://mentalhealth-uk.org/

12 things to remind yourself of every day

- The past cannot be changed
- Opinions do not define your reality or who you are
- Everyone's journey in life is different to yours
- Things will always get better with time
- Judgments are a confession of your character
- Overthinking often leads to sadness
- Happiness is found within
- Positive thoughts create positive outcomes
- Smiles are always contagious
- Kindness is 100% free
- You will only ever fail if you give up
- What goes around, comes around.

Here are a few inspiring quotes worth reading and remembering.

"Our greatest glory is not in falling,

but rising every time we fall"

Rocky Balboa

"Happiness can be found even in the darkest of times,

if one only remembers to turn on the light."

Albus Dumbledore

"There is a crack in everything,

that's how the light gets in."

Leonard Cohen

"Promise me you'll always remember:

You're braver than you believe,

and stronger than you seem,

and smarter than you think."

Christopher Robin

(Winnie the Pooh)

"Mental health problems don't define who you are.

They are something you experience.

You walk in the rain,

and you feel the rain,

but you are not the rain."

Matt Haig

Fishing Basics part 1

A guide to tackle and terminology

What is a Rig?

A 'rig' describes the tackle set up needed to catch fish, an example of this could be line with a float on it, a few weights, and a hook on the end. It could also be a ledgering setup, this is a weighted method that allows you to fish on the bottom. Other rigs could be the use of a feeder, which is an item of tackle that can be filled with groundbait or loose feed, in a similar style to ledgering, as that too is set up to catch from the bottom.

(See 'Rigs & Techniques' section for more information and examples)

What is Casting?

Casting is the action of launching your rig and bait into the water using a fishing rod and reel. There are several methods used to cast out rigs, most commonly, the overhead method, but also the underarm swing is a very good tactic for close in or on rivers.

What is Striking?

When you get a bite from a fish on your float, as an example, you must 'strike'. This pulls on the line and sets the hook into the fish's lip.

What is Playing a Fish?

When you strike and connect to a fish, you need to keep tension on the line to enable you to bring the fish in, as you reel in the line. This is done using functions on your reel and techniques to keep the tension on the line to avoid the hook coming out.

What is Landing a fish?

Once you have struck into a fish, played it, and brought it in near to the bank you are fishing from, you will then need to get it out of the water. This is done using a landing net, it allows you to scoop the fish out of the water so you can bring it in to unhook it with a disgorger or forceps.

What is Fish Welfare?

The welfare of the freshwater fish is paramount to the future of fishing and all fish that are caught must be returned to the water without injury. All fish are covered with a protective layer of slime, and this acts as the first line defence against parasitic infections, bacteria, and other diseases of a fish that it may contract. When you catch a fish, you must make sure you do not remove too much of this protective coating, so always wet your hands before handling the fish and never use a cloth to hold a fish. Always unhook fish quickly but carefully and return them to the water as quickly as possible. If the fish is too large to hold, use a wet unhooking mat on the ground. With smaller fish, hold them firmly so they do not flap about and slip out of your hands onto the ground, but do not hold them too tight or you may damage its internal organs.

What is fishing tackle?

In general terms, fishing tackle is the equipment an angler uses in the pursuit of fish.

A few examples of this are equipment like fishing rods, poles, whips, reels, fishing line, floats, hook, or weights. Hooks and weights are usually referred to as 'terminal' tackle, this includes things like swivels, snap links and other accessories that will be covered in this section.
Hundreds of years ago, fishing tackle was simple and consisted of just a line with a hook attached to the end of it. Over the years, fishing has been changed with the creation of things like poles, rods, reels, and thinner/stronger line. With the addition of this newer tackle, casting and fishing techniques have also changed considerably.

Fishing methods are also changing all the time, mostly for the better for the fish as well as the angler. If you are a beginner to fishing, you will be amazed at all the different types of fishing tackle available for the new angler.

What type of fishing tackle you will need always depends on a few things.

- The type of water you will be fishing, which could be anything from fast flowing or slow meandering rivers to lakes or small ponds.
- The species of fish you will be targeting like big carp or general coarse fish such as Roach or Bream.
- The methods of fishing you will be using like float fishing, feeder fishing, ledgering, or fly fishing.

What is a fishing rod?

The fishing rod is the main item of tackle used to cast out rigs and land fish. It is a pole with a handle, a connection point for a reel and a series of guide rings that the line is fed through. Several key elements of the rods strength and design features can often be confusing, so here are a few of them explained.

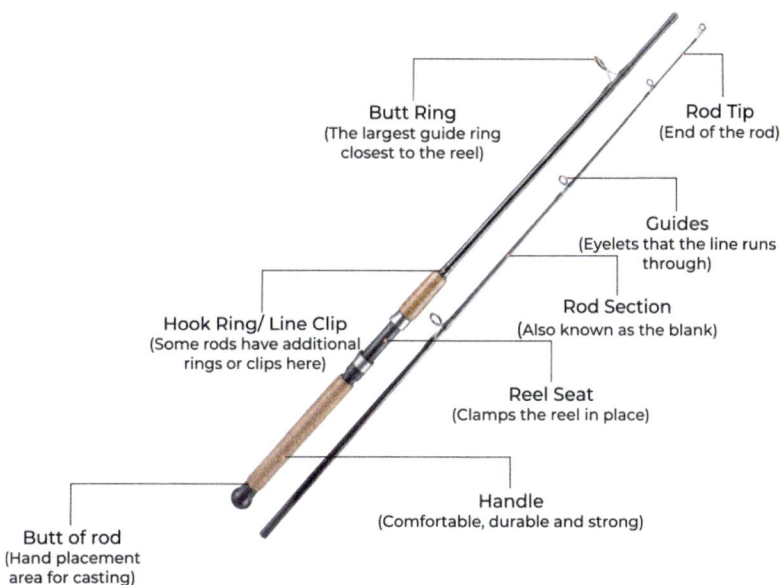

Butt Ring
(The largest guide ring closest to the reel)

Rod Tip
(End of the rod)

Guides
(Eyelets that the line runs through)

Hook Ring/ Line Clip
(Some rods have additional rings or clips here)

Rod Section
(Also known as the blank)

Reel Seat
(Clamps the reel in place)

Handle
(Comfortable, durable and strong)

Butt of rod
(Hand placement area for casting)

What is rod action?

Rod action is how the rod performs throughout its length, how it bends and reacts to casting weight or playing fish and also the amount of pressure it can withstand.

Fast action

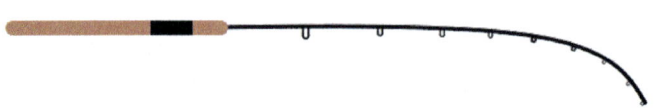

Fast action rods begin bending near the rod tip giving the angler great sensitivity and feel. A fast action rod will bend in the top third of the fishing rod. The added stiffness of a fast action rod means you do not have to move it very far on the hookset until the rod locks off and bends less in the middle.

Middle to tip action

These rods are a mixture of fast and through action, these are a jack of all trades covering most situations. This type of rod action is best suited for the beginner and often suitable for multiple styles of fishing.

Through action

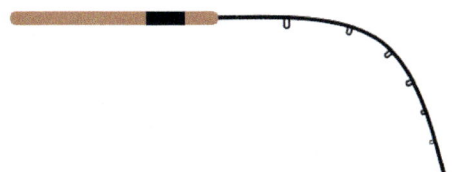

If you do not need to hit big distances, then a through action rod might just be the most satisfying to use when bringing fish to the bank. Good for short-range, surface and margin fishing with medium weight end tackle, but can lack backbone which means casting distances can be compromised.

What is test curve?

A test curve is a measurement, in pounds and ounces, of the weight needed to pull a rod tip through a 90-degree angle. Modern technology such as the use of carbon has created powerful rods that retain fish-playing finesse, whilst being strong enough to cast heavy weights.

All rods behave differently, and their characteristics are a mixture of their action and their test curve.

A few examples of a rod's test curve and the uses:

- **1lb to 2lb test curve** – These rods usually are aimed towards the specimen angler, when fishing for species such as big Chub, Tench, Barbel, and other large silver fish such as Bream.
  These rods will not be as strong as carp rods and provide more finesse when playing the larger specimen fish. They will also be limited on how much weight can be used on the rig, so maybe limited to casting weights of around 3-4oz.

- **2.25lb to 2.75lb test curve** – These rods are normally for larger weight casting, more so the bigger lead weights around 4-5 oz, but still provide a semi soft action to play fish with. Normally used for light carp fishing techniques such as stalking or floater fishing.

- **3lb-4lb test curve** – These rods can be specimen carp rods that can cast very large weights, normally 10ft or larger and have very big guide rings to allow for larger spooled reels and aid casting further distances. They can also be pike rods, for casting out large dead baits or playing large powerful fish.

- **4lb + test curve** – These rods are mostly used for something called 'spodding'. This is casting out large amounts of feed to create a big bed of bait when carp fishing. Spodding is when you cast out a device known as a 'spod' that large amounts of feed are stuffed into. When this hits the desired casting spot, it deploys the feed directly above the target area.

What fishing rod types are there?

There are several fishing rod types that you will see in shops, they all have their specific uses. When picking a certain style of fishing, you would need to be using the correct rod for the job. You would not want to go fishing for big Carp using a float fishing rod, or similarly using a Carp rod to go float fishing. They all have different actions, lengths, and even different types of guide/eyelets for the reel type used. The other reason for using the correct type of rod is also about protecting the fish and maintaining good fish welfare. A very stiff rod, when striking a small silver fish, would do some damage or even bounce the fish off the hook, so it is important and always best to use balanced tackle that's suitable.

Float fishing

These cover a broad range of float fishing requirements and normally have a medium action and most commonly range from 10ft to 14ft. There are many varieties of float rods, and these tend to match the floats being used in the rigs. A good example, and the most popular, is the waggler rod. These normally have quite soft rods that aid casting the floats out. There are also rods for stick floats, these tend to have a fast action but tend to be more sensitive to allow a more finesse style of fishing. Also, there are pellet waggler rods, which are slightly stiffer so they can cast out heavier floats.

Feeder/ledgering/quiver

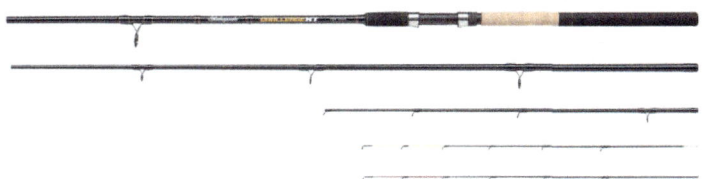

These come with several coloured tips that have different sensitivities dependant on what you are casting out and what sort of bite indication you need. Some tips are 1 - 3oz (Casting weight). These can range in size from 7ft to 13ft in size and vary a lot in strengths. Also known as quiver tip rods, and the coloured tips aid detecting bites from fish. The line is reeled in, so the tip is taught to the ledgered rig, so when a fish bites, it taps or bends the tip showing the bite.

Avon/Twin tip

These have lots of uses and are typically multi-function rods, these also come with multiple tip sections. Usually, one of the tips is like a float rod, although a lot stronger, with a test curve from 1lb to 2lb. Other tips are usually strong quiver tips that range from 1oz to 5oz. These tend to be for specialist use when fishing for specimen fish on large rivers or lakes.

Carp fishing

These are rods specifically designed for large fish, big baits, and strong line. They come in many different strengths and lengths, but 12ft is traditionally the most common rod length. For the ultimate long-distance casting rods, you will need 13ft, since this creates a bigger lever effect and will propel your rig further. Stalker rods are considered a specialist tool and they range from 6ft to 10ft in length, making them perfect for poking into the smallest gaps in the foliage. It is particularly important as a carp angler to have the right specifications on your carp rods.

Lure/Spinning/Predator fishing

Lure rods or spinning rods for pike and predator fishing come in a wide range of lengths and casting weights, all suited for different applications. Casting weights can range from as little as 0.5g to over 200g. Rods with lighter casting weights are designed for casting small lures and dropshot rigs for species such as Perch and are soft to allow the jigging or twitching of the lure baits. Some predator fishing rods, such as Pike rods, tend to be for dead baiting and are very similar to Carp rods.

Fly Fishing

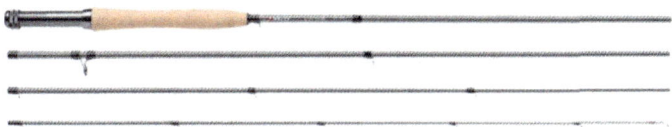

A fly rod in broad principle, is made like any other fishing rod, but there are some major differences. The rod is typically very lightweight and thin compared to most fishing rods. Fly rods are classified like lure or spinning rods after length and the weight they are supposed to cast. Unlike lure or spinning rods, the weight is that of the line and not of the lure, since it is the line that is used to cast the very light fly and it's the line that requires a suitable rod to cast well. The other noticeable difference is the lack of handle at the butt end of the rod, the reel is positioned at the lowest point. This is to help reduce weight, and also because the fly-casting action is completely different.

What is a fishing reel?

A fishing reel is a device mounted on to the butt (handle) of a fishing rod and holds the fishing line. It is used for casting and retrieving the
fishing line. There are many different types of fishing reels, and each reel is designed to be used for a specific type of fishing.

Fixed spool reel

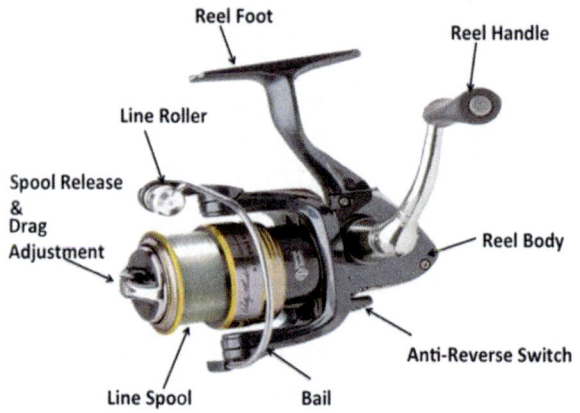

Front Drag Model

The most used fishing reel in coarse fishing. The line roller rotates with the handle, the spool is geared to move up and down during rotation. This wraps the line around the spool neatly. Most modern-day reels all come with some form of drag control, this is used to adjust the tension on the spool. When you are playing a fish and landing it, some large or powerful fish will take line of the reel, having this tension reduced so it can do so with a little force reduces the chance of line breakage or hooks coming out.

The reel in the first image is a 'Front Drag' model, so the drag adjustment is a dial on the front of the spool.

Some models can also come with the drag on the rear of the reel (shown below) and this is called 'Rear Drag'.

Rear Drag model

The rear drag reels also have a quick release spool via a push button. To remove the spool on a front drag reel, the drag adjustment dial has to be completely unwound and removed.

Some specimen reels also have a free spool function (Such as Shimano's 'baitrunner') and this is a secondary drag setting with even lower tension, used in conjunction with bite alarms.

 *This can be switched off back to normal settings when playing a fish via a switch or lever.*

What are the reel sizes?

You'll find that reels have a number series on them, as an example 3000 or 30. This denotes the size of the reel and the capacity of the spool.

1000 / 2000

These are for short distance and low diameter line, these reels are small and generally for light work (Small ponds or canals). Generally, casting can be up to 20m, as they tend to be used with smaller/lighter rigs and also the spools are smaller.

3000

This is the most common sized reel used for float fishing on commercials or lakes at medium range, casting anything up to 30m. Perfect for waggler fishing with 4-5lb line. This reel can also be used for light ledgering work or light feeder work on streams and small rivers.

4000

These sized reels usually have a faster line retrieve, larger capacity spools for lines from 5- 8lb being ideal. Perfect for feeder fishing up to around 40m range, with either method or groundbait feeders, but also good for ledgering work.

5000

These reels are for hitting long distances, a great tool for targeting Barbel, Chub, or large Bream. Good for the heavier, stronger line, long distance casting or heavy river work.

6000 / 8000 / 10000

These reels have huge spools for long distance work and larger diameter lines and braids. Primarily these are Carp reels but are also used for all large species fish such as Catfish. Fast retrieving gear ratios mean that long distance casting can be reeled back in quickly. These reels also are better equipped to handle larger fish with more robust drag systems and stronger gearing.

Centre pin reel

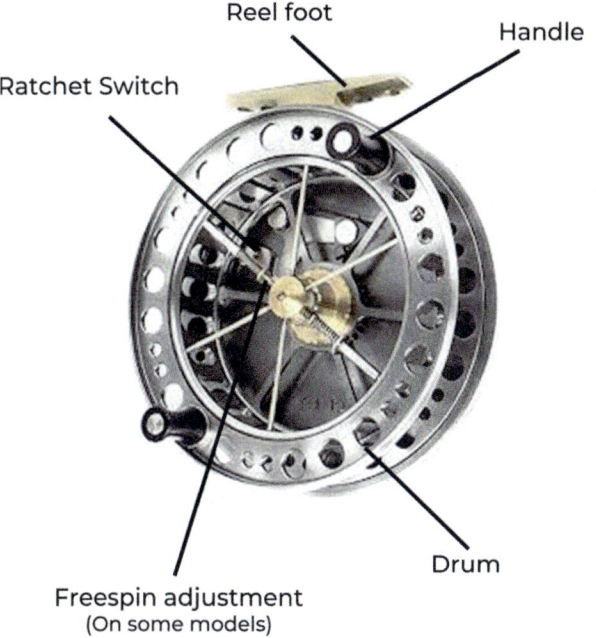

Some anglers say it is a great reel for trotting a float down a fast-flowing river. Its function has been slightly superseded by the closed face reel but the feeling of a centrepin reel cannot be imitated. The connection you feel when a fish takes the bait is unsurpassed. Some models have a ratchet switch, which when engaged allows the angler to control the line release when trotting, giving the ability to have inch by inch control. It can also act as a basic form of drag, as it impedes the flow of line from the reel adding pressure. With the models featuring the ratchet switch they can also be used for ledger or feeder fishing or freelining baits.

Closed face reel

This type of reel is also very similar in function to the fixed spool reel with a few exceptions. The spool has a cover and there is no bail arm or line runner. To cast it is as simple as pressing the bail pin(s) which lets the line run freely off the spool, then with another touch of the finger the line can be stopped, having the same effect as closing the bail arm on a fixed spool reel. This type of reel is very popular with some anglers due to its simplicity and its ability to avoid line tangles, especially in windy conditions.

What it a rod rest?

A rod rest is an essential piece of kit for any angler, whether you are just resting your float rod on it whilst you wait for a bite, or those who are using it for a quiver tip rod.

Using rod rests for float rods isn't always needed but it can help in keeping the hands free for doing other things like making up groundbait or tying other rigs.

When using it for feeder fishing, ledgering with a quivertip or similar, the rod rest comes into its own, allowing the angler to keep the rod still so the tip of the rod can be used to detect bites. There are many types of rod rests, some are just the rest that screws into a bank stick (this is a pole that can be pressed into the ground with a fitting on top for multiple rest adapters), and some are purpose made. They are a worthwhile addition to any angler's setup and provides a simple alternative to using alarms and receivers.

What is a rod pod?

This is basically a setup of 2 or 3 rod rests for both the butt of the rod and the blank (just before or after the butt ring). This allows anglers, mainly specimen anglers, to use bite alarm setups. These are a great way to allow the angler to detect bites that take a while to develop and keeping 2 or 3 rods neatly in close together, helps to keep the swim tidy and safer.

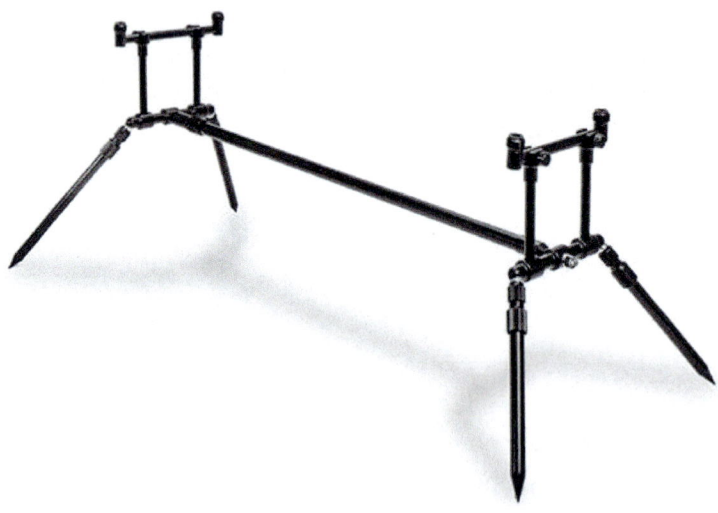

What is a bite alarm?

This is a piece of kit that detects the line moving on a roller, this movement triggers an audible sounder. The line is fed from the reel, rests on the alarm roller and is held with a little tension often by bobbins or swingers. These add a little resistance to the line when being used with a bite alarm, so the line is in constant contact with the alarm roller. The ringed clamp part of the swinger is fitted onto the thread of the alarm and is then camped in place when the alarm is tightened down to the bank stick adapter.

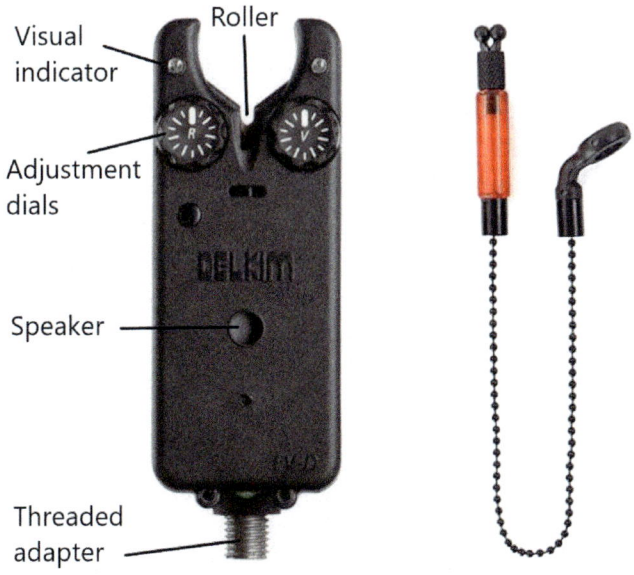

What is a pole?

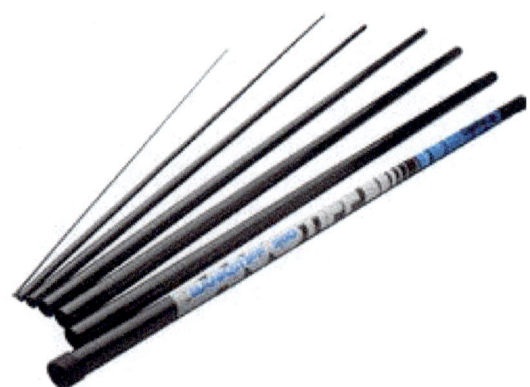

A pole is a fishing tool, like a fishing rod but, with no guides/eyelets. A pole doesn't use a reel, it has an elasticated section that elastic is fed through. Your line is then connected to the end of this elastic which has a connector at the tip end. The other end of the elastic is tethered internally to a bung. This is usually the top 2-3 sections only. Some can be as long as 16m. These are used for reaching distant spots in lakes and rivers, for example, and are not the easiest to handle if you don't have the experience. They are, however, very effective, and can bring excellent results if you use them correctly. Apart from the top 3, the rest of the pole is made of sections that fit inside each other, these are then connected together and fed through the hands. More sections are added until the correct length is required. Rigs for these are kept on winders, premade and ready to go.

What is a whip?

A whip is a smaller, often telescopic, version of a fishing pole. Because it is compact, this makes it easier for anglers to carry around. A fishing whip is usually around 2-5m long and are perfect for beginners, as there is minimal setup needed. The main difference between a pole and a whip, is mainly the top sections of poles are elasticated, whereas some whips maybe elasticated they primarily come with quick connectors that are bonded to the tip (known as a 'Stonfo' connector).

What is a terminal tackle?

Hooks and weights are the main elements of what is widely known as 'Terminal Tackle,' but also there are connection or jointing items that are used when making a rig.

Hooks

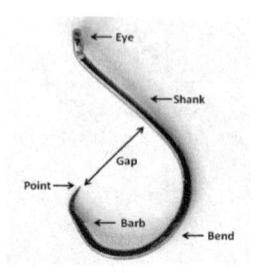

This is your final and critical link to catching a fish, it is used to pierce the mouth of a fish when they take the bait, or a bite is struck into. They range from sizes 24 (Small) to 2 (Large) in coarse, specimen and carp fishing. There are many different patterns and shapes specifically designed work with certain rig methods. Most hooks are connected and tied via the eye that is forged into them, but some hooks (Smaller sizes below 16 mostly) can have something called a 'Spade end'. This requires a different knot to attach it with and there are very useful knot tying tools to use for this job.

Split Shot

A spherical soft weight with a groove running through it, the line is put into the groove and the shot is then pinched tight to hold it in position. They are used to set the depth of a float's buoyancy and sometimes used in a pattern to aid bait presentation.

If you find the sizes and weights confusing, us the conversion chart to help you when making rigs or shotting patterns for float fishing.

\multicolumn{3}{c	}{CONVERSION CHART}
Split Shot Size	Weight (g)	Equivalent
3 SSG	4.8g	6x AAA
2 SSG	3.2g	4x AAA
LG	3g	
LSG	2g	
SSG	1.6g	2x AAA
AAA	0.8g	2x BB
AB	0.6g	2x No 1
BB	0.4g	2x No 4
No 1	0.3g	2x No 5
No 3	0.25g	
No 4	0.2g	2x No 6
No 5	0.15g	
No 6	0.1g	2x No 9
No 8	0.06g	2x No 11
No 9	0.05g	
No 10	0.04g	2x No12
No 11	0.03g	
No 12	0.02g	2x No 13
No 13	0.01g	

There are also types of shot called 'Stots' and these are a similar weight but are more of a cylindrical shape that are designed primarily for the lighter pole floats.

Ledgering Weights

These are used to pin the line and bait to the floor of the area where you are fishing. Often these are used with lead clip systems when carp fishing or using as a bolt rig, but there are other methods where you attach them on run-rings when a non-static approach is needed. This allows the weight to move freely on the line, removing the bolt rig effect, as this can sometimes spook a fish. They can range in sizes from 1 oz to over 4 oz, the smallest sizes are usually used for close in or light ledgering rigs. The larger weights are used for larger fish, such as Carp, fishing at long distances or in high current flow to help pin the rig to the bottom.

Swivels and other connectors

These are used at the end of your mainline to connect hook lengths or sometimes to create special rigs for items such as feeders. They come in all shapes and sizes and swivels can also reduce line twist. Some swivels have the ring on one side and another type of connector on the other, and these are specifically designed for quick connection of other parts of the rig or hook lengths. There are also items used within the specimen fishing methods, such as bait screws or maggot rings. These are a more specialist item, and often are used to attach boiled baits or large amounts of hook bait to tempt the larger species.

The most used connectors for attaching things like hook lengths are quick to change, this is to reduce the need to break down tackle or untangle the commonly used loop to loop knot.

Most popular connectors for this are things like, quick change beads, this is a bead shaped item that can be pulled apart to reveal connection points for loops or can be tied to the mainline.

These are just a few items that can be used, there are many manufacturers that produce connectors for this specific requirement, so it almost will be a personal preference rather than one being superior to the other.

Swim feeders and leads can be attached to the line using a variety of connectors or knots. The old style was using something called a 4-turn water knot to attach them with a link made of weaker line. Nowadays, we have lots of quick connectors to choose from.

Most popular is the quick-change run ring, basically a plastic-coated big eye with a snap link on it. This allows the feeder to move up and down the line easily in case of snags or to cope with flow characteristics of the waters current.

Others use the same connectors they use in carp fishing, something called a 'Lead Clip'. Normally for the bolt rig affect but also allows the feeder to be dislodged if snagged but can be used in a sliding fashion.

What are feeders?

For fishing in freshwater, a feeder is a great way of presenting groundbait or loose feed close to where your hook bait lies. These are weighted, so no other weights are needed. These come any many shapes and sizes, as well as types.

Maggot feeder

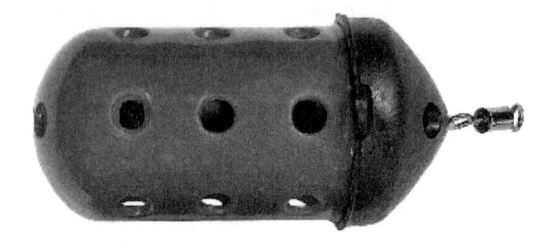

This is usually a capped plastic feeder with lots of holes in it, and loose feed or maggots are packed in. The holes allow the feed to slowly release or escape into the area you are fishing.

Open end/Groundbait feeder

This is a feeder with an outer with holes, like the maggot feeder, but larger. This allows groundbait to be packed into it and are good for casting and accurately placing the feed in the area.

Cage feeder

A feeder made with a mesh outer, similar use as the open end/groundbait feeder, this can hold groundbait and helps to release it easily in the waters flow.

Method feeder

Groundbait or soaked pellet packed on to the frame and hook bait can be tucked into it before casting for better presentation. This type of feeder uses a short hooklink.

Hybrid feeder

This is the same as the method feeder, only the feeder itself is a cross between a flat ledgering weight and the method feeder. As with the method feeder, this also uses a short hooklength.

What is float fishing?

Float fishing is one of the most popular and probably one of easiest ways to catch a wide variety of fish from lakes, ponds, rivers, and streams. This is a method of fishing that involves suspending a bait underneath a float. Floats do vary in shapes, material, and styles but all perform the same basic task of bite detection. The tip has highly visible paint to aid bite indication, so it can be seen from distance. When float fishing, the angler is watching the float tip for any activity below, waiting for it to dip under the surface when a fish takes the bait. Since no terminal tackle is in contact with the bottom (unless fished over depth), the float is free from being snagged. Although when river fishing, or fishing moving waters, it can indicate the bait or hook dragging on the bottom if the float's tip dips as it moves with the flow.

Float fishing requires you to set the depth you want to fish, how you want your bait to be presented and in what way. The method in which you set the depth of a float, so it is at the bottom of the lake or river etc, is called 'plumbing the depth.' When setting up any float rig, it is always a good idea to plumb the depth, this allows you to check your swim for more information on how deep it is below the surface. It is always a good starting point, as more experienced anglers change the depth and style to which they suspend their bait under the float.

What is a float?

A float provides a visual indication of when a fish bites and takes your bait. On every float, on the side is the amount of weight needed to cock it correctly, so the tip is showing when in the water. There are 3 main types of floats used, waggler, stick and the floats used with fishing poles but there are many more and they all do a specific job.

Waggler

This is the most common form of float for fishing and is very easy to set up and use as it is only attached at the bottom end. Used on still waters such as lakes and canals but can be used on the river if the flow is not too fast. These floats are also made of different materials such as peacock quill (Peacock Waggler) or clear tubing (Crystal waggler). They can come with a body on bottom end (bodied waggler) and are useful on lakes that have moving water surface.

Stick

Has an elongated body and attached via three float rubbers. Used on running water such as rivers with methods such as stret-pegging and trotting. The tips are normally very short, so often help detect the slightest of bites. The floats depth is set by the float rubbers and plumbing the depth (or using other methods).

Pole

Very sensitive and held in place by tiny rubber sleeves. Come in many different shapes. There are Pear shaped ones for any water, dibbers (small ones) for shallow waters and 'body up' shapes for running water. The tip is called the bristle, the wider part is called the body, and this is what makes it buoyant. Then there is the stick part which is called the stem. There are three types of pole float stem, and these are carbon, fibreglass, and wire.

Pellet waggler

A pellet waggler is a float used for any small particle baits. It can also be used for larger baits such as cut cubes of meat. Its main use is to present a bait near the surface of the water, usually in the top 2". They come in many shapes and sizes, usually loaded with large amounts of weight, and tend to have a very visible top to aid bite detection at distance.

Avon float

An alloy stemmed stick float designed for fishing at close range in fast water, the float being controlled in much the same fashion as a shouldered stick float. The shoulder allows for holding back slowing the hook bait, although it can be extremely effective when allowed to run through at the same speed as the flow.

Drift beater

Drift beaters are designed for anchoring baits on the bottom in still waters. Lift bites can be produced by over-shotting with big anchor shot on the lakebed, and with the buoyant sight bob just riding at the surface. The long thin Fibre Glass stem is ideal for getting below surface drift on big, open waters where stability and good visibility is required.

Loafer/Chubber

These floats can be used with everything from trotting bread and maggots for roach and chub to fishing small fish baits for species like perch. Their buoyancy offers excellent visibility in turbulent water and help to control weighty baits like luncheon meat or large lob worms. Used in the same principles as a waggler, and sometimes used with a float rubber on the tip section.

What do we need to get the fish out of the water?

Now we know more about the tackle used to catch fish, let's look at what we need to get them out of the water safely, unhook them and protect them. It's worthwhile taking a visit to your local tackle shop when looking for the correct kit, as some of the things may not be necessary for your target species and they can advise you with current products. For instance, you won't need an unhooking mat for small silver fish, at the same time you won't be able to use a small spoon landing net for a 20lb Carp.

What is an unhooking mat?

An unhooking mat is a large, padded cushion to protect fish from being injured on the ground or any rough surfaces.

What is a landing net?

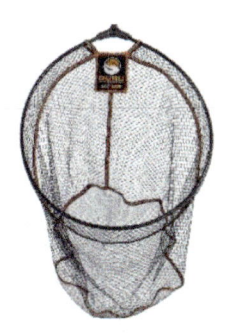

A landing net is a soft mesh net that is reinforced with a metal ring to keep its shape, this is then attached to a handle. Landing nets come in so many different shapes and sizes like small pan nets for coarse fish, large nets for specimen and fold up nets for predatory fish as examples. Some handles are a single piece, some are also telescopic, again there are many different types to choose from.

What is a disgorger?

The disgorger is a thin plastic or metal rod with a slot in the end specially designed to remove hooks.

What are forceps?

Forceps are for when you are using large hooks or unhooking fish that have sharp teeth, but sometimes can help if you are struggling with a disgorger.

What is a keepnet?

A keepnet is used to keep fish you have caught in a contained area. It is basically a netted tunnel with an entry point that is fixed to a rod rest pole. Its more popular with match anglers as they have to keep a tally or total weight of their fish to win. Fish that are being released back into the water, after a while will spook off the fish in your swim, more so if they are part of the shoal. It is advised by most clubs and venue owners that Carp are kept in separate keepnets, and no fish is kept in a keepnet longer than 6 hours, less if the water temperature is high. So be considerate during warmer weather, probably best not to use one.

What kit do you need to get started?

This all depends on what type of fishing you wish to do or try. The most rewarding way any new angler can start with is float fishing. It is a simple way to fish and can get you catching fish straight away. What fishing kit do we need to actually catch fish? apart from things like bait tubs, hand towels, a bag to put all the bits in and other niceties like chairs, what do we need to buy?

Top tip! Remember ask angling societies and clubs, as they will always try to help members with donated tackle or cheap used tackle.

What do I need to go float fishing with a whip or pole?

Whip fishing kits are widely available from all good tackle stores for a very low price. Most whip fishing kits have everything you need to go fishing. They include a 3m – 4m pole, a premade rig on a winder and a disgorger, so all you would need is a landing net and bait!

Top tip! Check out the Angling Trust website for more information on where you can find Get Fishing events, at these events you can learn how to use the kit. Also look out for discounts online during nation fishing month.

What do I need to go float fishing with a rod and reel?

The kit you need differs a lot when fishing with rod and reel, there will be a few more bits you will need to get before you can start.

Float fishing rod - 10ft to 11ft

Fixed spool reel
size 2500 - 3000

Fishing line
5lb (0.20mm)

Landing net
and handle

Pack of floats
(mixed variety)

Disgorger
set

Pair of scissors

Split shot

Hooklengths
(Hooks to nylon)

Quick change
swivels

51

Fishing Basics part 2

A guide to the basic techniques used in fishing

What is watercraft?

Watercraft is how and where to find your target species of fish. It is learning and developing the ability to analyse the venue. It enables you to determine where the fish are likely to be, according to different aspects and scenarios such as the weather, feeding patterns, wind direction, and pressure. This is a skill that needs to be learned over many years and can only be developed by spending time on the bank or your venue, learning from failures and results.

Most anglers understand that there is a need to learn more about watercraft, but very few actually every truly master the skill. Lots of anglers do not catch any fish (known as a 'blank' or 'blanking') on fishing sessions simply because they are ignoring the signs of feeding fish and fail to follow the fish around the lake.

Whenever you are applying watercraft, you will find that what works on one venue, doesn't work on another venue, they are all different in terms of feeding habits, holding spots and how the weather affects the water. But one thing that is consistent with every venue, is that you need to find the fish before you can catch them. If they aren't in your swim, it's unlikely that you will catch them.

Location is the most important aspect when it comes to fishing. If you are in the wrong swim because the fish are elsewhere, then the chances of catching them are very low. The key to finding the fish is using the skills of watercraft to look for feeding fish, or fish holding up in particular parts of the venue. This is what anglers describe as watercraft. Most species of fish try to avoid predation, so under trees, Lilly beds, in front of reeds are always very good places to start. Anywhere that looks covered of sheltered are great spots to catch fish, although at risk of being snagged up.

There are certain things to look for in certain species, that give away their position. Species such as Roach, Rudd, and other small silver fish, do not tend to give many indications that they are there. Finding these fish is more to do with locating habitat and areas where they shoal up (In a large group) and being a shoaling fish, this is quite common.

Species such as Carp, Tench, and Bream give away different indications. The main one is something called 'Bubbling'. This is when you see bubbling or fizzing on the water's surface. This indicates that there are fish feeding below. It is where they are disturbing gasses that are being released from the silt or the bottom of lake or pond, and also gasses being pushed out through the fish's gills. Sometimes the lakebed can release gasses, but these generally are always in the same spot. If the bubbling moves, it's a fish feeding. Also look for cloudy patches of water, this gives of a sign that feeding has taken place. Flanking could also be another reason for bubbles, this happens when Carp are cleaning themselves off. They do this by rubbing the sides of their bodies against the lakebed, this could then be followed by them jumping out of the water, called 'showing' or 'crashing'. Flanking will result in a much larger sheet of bubbles on the lake surface, almost like an eruption, which is commonly known as "sheeting up".

(See 'Fish Facts' section for more information and examples)

How to setup a fishing rod and reel

To start fishing you will need to know the basic (but one of the most important) thing, how to put together a rod and attaching a reel. It is important that this is done correctly, as the rod could come apart or become damaged if not connected properly or not cast very well if the guide rings/eyelets are not in line with each other. Also, the reel could fall off and possibly cause injury or damage.

How to put a rod together

Carefully remove the rod from is protective sling, placing each section carefully down on the ground or away from anyway where it could get damaged. Most commonly, rods come with either 3 sections (butt/middle/tip) and some have 2 sections (butt/tip).

Take the tip section first, this is the thinnest section, and dependant on how many sections you have, either connect this to the spigot of the middle section or if a 2 piece, attach it to the butt section.

Top Tip! You may find during the summer months they may be hard to get apart when breaking down, so using the colder water in the lake, wet the join to help cool it down or keep it out of the sun for a while.

Gently push them together and align the guides, then push it in a little further to secure it. It does not need to be rammed in, but just secure enough that it will not come off.

Important Safety Tip! Please remember that fishing rods are conductive, this means that they are very good electrical conductors. If you are going fishing and a storm is approaching or are planning to go and it is forecasted to happen, pack up and leave or simply do not go.

How to attach a reel to the rod

To fit a reel to the rod, we need to clamp it in place to the reel seat on the butt section of the rod. Some rods have a fixed top clamp and a lower securing clamp that screws into position. Other/older rods have reel securing clamp rings that run loose on the handle of the rod, these need to be moved so that the top one is around 3 to 4 inches away from the top of the handle (or the same as the width of your hand). And the reel foot is forced into the top and the lower one is wound/forced over the lower part of the foot to lock it into position. As most modern rods have a screw fitting, the guide will be based on that.

Insert the foot into the fixed part of the clamp on the reel seat.

Then adjust foot to be in line with the second clamp and screw into place. Check the alignment of reel to rod guides/eyelets.

How to load line onto a reel

Before you can do anything with a rod and reel, you will need to put some line onto the reel so you can set up rigs etc. The line strength depends on what you intend to do fishing wise, are you float fishing for general fish? or river fishing for chub?

(See 'Fish Facts' section for more information)

Once you have checked what sort of line strength you will need, you will now need to get it on to the spool of the reel.

Using the same techniques as previous shown, connect the reel to the butt section of the rod and turn on the anti-reverse switch.

You will need a hand towel or flannel, a bowl of water and a jar of jam or a tin of beans or something similar.

Remove the band that is on the spool of line or whatever is holding the line in place and pull off a few metres of line and feed the line backwards, though the butt ring towards the reel.

Now you will need to tie an Arbor knot.

(See 'Knot Knowledge' section for more information on how to do this)

Open the bail arm and feed the loop of the arbour knot over the spool and tighten it down, now close the bail arm.

Place the bowl of water on a table or floor, now and put the spool of line into the water.

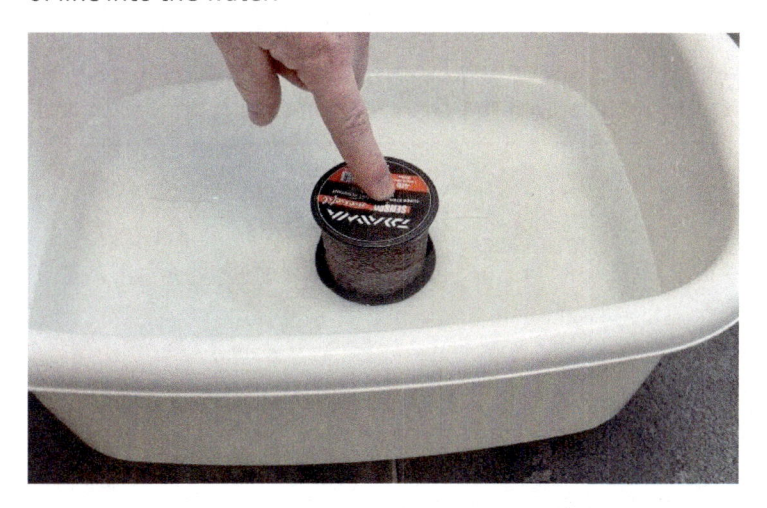

Now place the jam jar/tin of beans on top, this will stop the spool of line from moving.

Using the hand towel or flannel, place it in your hand and slightly hold the line to the rod blank just above or below the butt ring (whichever is more comfortable). This will help create tension between the line and the reel spool, it ensures a good line lay on the reel to help reduce the chance of line being too loose and tangling.

Position the butt ring over the spool in the bowl of water as best as you can.

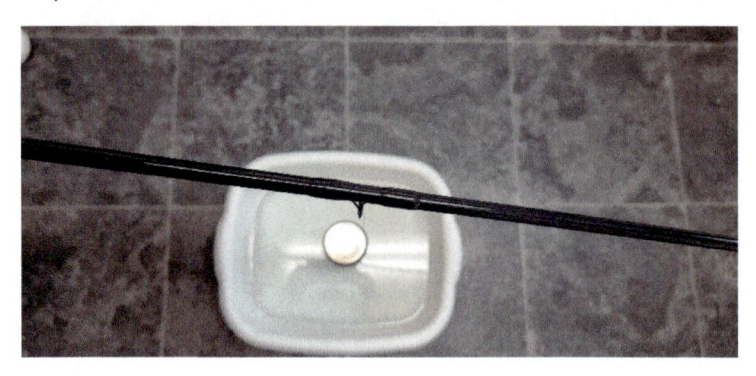

Now reel it in until the line is around 2mm from the edge of the reel spool lip.

Trap the line into the line clip on the reel spool or trap in place using an elastic band or hair band. Clear everything up and you are ready to go!

How to set the rod up ready for a rig

Now you have both rod and reel attached (loaded with line), you'll need to feed the line through the guide rings so it's ready to start making a rig.

Firstly, make sure the anti-reverse switch is on, this will make sure that any pulling on the line doesn't result into the reel spinning frantically letting lots of line off the spool or causing a tangle.

The most efficient way to take line off the spool of the reel without causing tangles, is to use the drag. Set the drag loose, so you can spin the spool by hand with minimal effort . not too loose though, as with front drag reels, the drag is also the securing bolt for the spool.

Now you will need to open the bail arm, unclip the line or find the end of the line. Pull around a metre off the spool and close the bail arm.

With one hand hold the rod near the butt ring, and with the other hand carefully feed the line through the butt ring, ensuring once it's through, move the hand holding the rod past the ring and clamp the line with a finger.

Now taking the line, and releasing the finger you clamped with, move up to the next ring. Move the hand that is holding the rod into the position just before the guide ring you are feeding it through and repeat the previous steps. Feeding it through and clamping it with a finger.

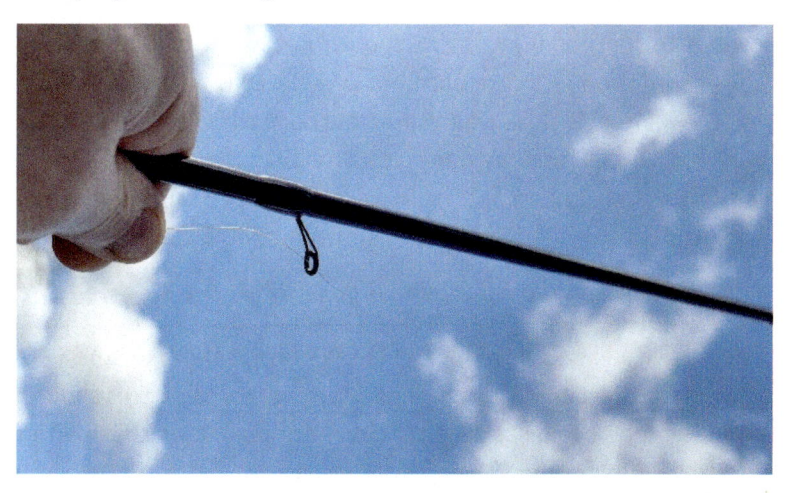

Repeat this all the way up the rod until it is out of the tip ring. Take more time and care with how you keep hold of the line as you feed it nearer the top, this is a lot more difficult with smaller guides. Now pull the line down towards the butt of the rod. This will now enable you to put the rod in a rod rest or carefully on the floor and give you enough line to start working on your rig with.

(See 'Rigs & Techniques' section for more on setting up rigs)

Once the rig is tied and the rod is ready to use, make sure you have readjusted your drag, so it is set ready for use. This should be set so that it takes a decent amount of pulling on the line for it to take line off or get the spool spinning.

How to cast – Overhead method

Top Tip! Make sure there are no trees or other obstacles behind you!

Once you have your rod setup and rig tied with bait on, you now want to get it onto your desired spot. Have a practice with just a rod and reel first until you get the feel of the actions.

Hold the rod with one hand near the reel and the other near the butt of the rod. Some people like to have the reel's foot in between their fingers, others with their hand just in front of the reel foot.

Think of a clock's positions (with 12 o'clock pointing straight up and 9 o'clock right behind you and 3 o'clock directly in front of you). Point the top of the rod to 2 o'clock in front of you and towards your target spot. Ensure there is enough line so that your float/ledger is around 2 ft from the rod tip.

Make sure the line roller is positioned upwards towards the rod (the part of the reel where the line exits the spool). Use your forefinger to trap the line against the rod blank to stop any line coming off (some people also like to trap the line in between the forefinger and the rim of the spool).

Now, with your other hand, open the bail arm of the reel so the line is now free. If you need to make any adjustments, it is best to close the bail arm and start the process again (this stops line coming off the spool freely as it can cause knots and tangles).

Move the rod backwards, slightly to the side of your shoulder (this helps to stop the rig tangling with the rod) and over your head, move it to the 10 o'clock position and let your rig hang steady. Your top hand should be just aside your ear.

Now with an overhead motion (almost pivoting from your lowest hand), punch/flick the rod forward and stop at the 2 o'clock position.

Top Tip! Try to get your rig just past your desired spot, as you will need to remove line slack at the end of your cast and potentially sink the line. By doing this it will cause the rig to move towards you.

This needs to be a smooth motion almost pivoting from the lower hand. Just before the 2 o'clock position is reached (around 1 o'clock), remove your finger from the spool to let your rig fly out and pull line off the reel.

Just before it hits the water, lower your rod parallel with the water and put your finger across the side of the spool lip to stop the line coming off and to help slow it down (this can help set the rigs position and reduce water disturbance). This should cause your rig to fall into the water in a straight line with the hook furthest from you.

Close the bail arm, now dip the rod tip under the water and slowly reel in to where you intend to fish. Doing this will sink the line and help stop your float drifting with the wind blowing across the top surface of the water.

How to cast – Underarm method

This is very similar to fishing the short pole or whip and is simply swinging out the rig with a slight flick whilst the bail arm is open.

Hold the rod with one hand near the reel and the other near the butt of the rod. Some people like to have the reel's foot in between their fingers, others with their hand just in front of the reel foot.

Think of a clock's positions (with 12 o'clock pointing straight up and 9 o'clock right behind you and 3 o'clock directly in front of you). Point the top of the rod to 2 o'clock in front of you and towards your target spot. Ensure there is enough line so that your float/ledger is around 1 metre from the rod tip, it will need to be longer than the other head cast as it'll need enough length to swing with.

Make sure the line roller is positioned upwards towards the rod (the part of the reel where the line exits the spool). Use your forefinger to trap the line against the rod blank to stop any line coming off (some people also like to trap the line in between the forefinger and the rim of the spool).

 Now, with your other hand, open the bail arm of the reel so the line is now free. If you need to make any adjustments, it is best to close the bail arm and start the process again (this stops line coming off the spool freely as it can cause knots and tangles).

Using a pendulum type motion (lowest hand is almost a pivot point), swing the rig in towards you.

Tilt the rod tip down slightly in front of you and then swing it back out. When the rig swings past underneath the rod's tip (the same position as it is hanging freely from the tip), tilt the rod up slightly at the same time as using a flicking action and release the line.

Top Tip! Try to get your rig just past your desired spot, as you will need to remove line slack at the end of your cast and potentially sink the line. By doing this it will cause the rig to move towards you.

Just before it hits the water, lower your rod parallel with the water and put your finger across the side of the spool lip to stop the line coming off and to help slow it down (this can help set the rigs position and reduce water disturbance). This should cause your rig to fall into the water in a straight line with the hook furthest from you.

Close the bail arm, now dip the rod tip under the water and slowly reel in to where you intend to fish. Doing this will sink the line and help stop your float drifting with the wind blowing across the top surface of the water.

Top Tip! If you are float fishing, it can sometimes pay to chuck out a few pinches of loose feed or hook baits on the spot before casting. This will help to get the fish more confident feeding, and less spooked by the noise of the rig landing in the water.

How to strike and play the fish

Holding your rod near the reel and in one swift movement lift it up in an arc pointing the tip slightly upwards until you feel the resistance of the fish. If you can feel resistance on the line, you have hooked the fish. When striking, as soon as you feel resistance try not to pull too hard when lifting your rod, you could pull the hook out of the fish or snap the line. **Always keep tension on the line** when playing a fish.

Keeping the line taut, start to reel in and at the same time lower the rod tip towards the water so there is a slight angle between rod and line - do not point the rod straight at the fish. Once you get to this point, you can then gently ease the rod back into pulling the fish in, keeping the bend in the tip. This process is repeat seral times until the fish is close in and showing signs of being tired or surfacing.

Playing a fish using drag

If it is a small fish, you will be able to reel it in and use your landing net, or if very small, you can just swing it in directly into your hand (The same you would a whip or pole). With a large fish you may need to keep the line taut but let the fish swim about and tire itself out first as you try to reel it in. If it starts to swim away from you, trying to pull line off the reel, there is only two options. Firstly, and the easiest way to do it is to use the drag system, this is an action that is controlled by the drag settings on your reel, some are at the front of the spool (Front drag), and some are at the rear of the reel (Rear drag). This is a dial adjustment that allows you to set the tension of how much force is needed to take line off the reel.

The other method is to use backwind techniques. This is when you disengage the anti-reverse switch on your reel that allows you to wind the opposite way. You can then manually control how much line the fish can take, but this requires a good level of skill and experience on how the fish may behave.

Have a play with the reel and test the settings to understand how it works, pulling on the line enables you to work out the tension needed (with practice). If the fish is taking line to quickly and a lot more than you can reel it in, tighten the drag a little more.

Be careful not to tighten it too much, if it is a large fish, the line will either snap or you could injure the fish.

You can also put your finger on the spool to stop the line if it starts swimming too far away, this gives you an opportunity to adjust the drag. You will learn through experience when to do this, as with each strength of line or size of fish drastically changes how much drag is needed.

How to land a fish

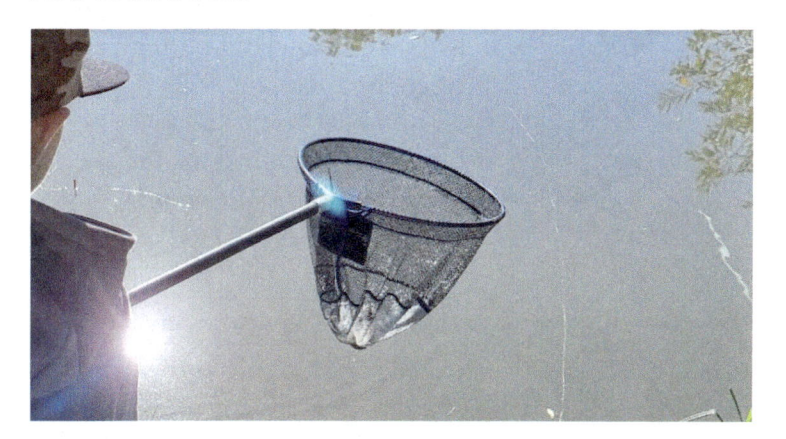

When you have reeled the fish in close enough so that it can be reached with your landing net, hold the handle of your landing net, and place the net in the water so it is completely submerged. Using your rod and remembering to keep the line taut, guide the fish to your net. When the fish is over your net lift it up to trap the fish. A small fish can be lifted out of the water. With a big fish, once it is in the net, you will have to pull the net through the water closer to the bank and lift the fish out of the water holding the sides of the net.

Unhooking a fish

Never pull on the line to remove a hook from a fish, you will end up seriously injuring the fish or breaking the line. If the fish is too large to hold in one hand, lay it on a wet unhooking mat to remove the hook.

If the fish is lip hooked, you may be able to remove it with your fingers. If the fish is hooked inside its mouth and you can see the hook, use a tool called a disgorger or forceps.

How to use a disgorger

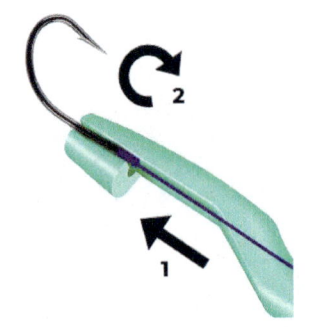

1. Hold the line tight and put the slot of the disgorger over the line and slide it along the line until you reach the hook.
2. Push it downwards so the point comes out and turn it, so the hook is in the opposite direction to the way it went in. Once it is free, carefully remove it.

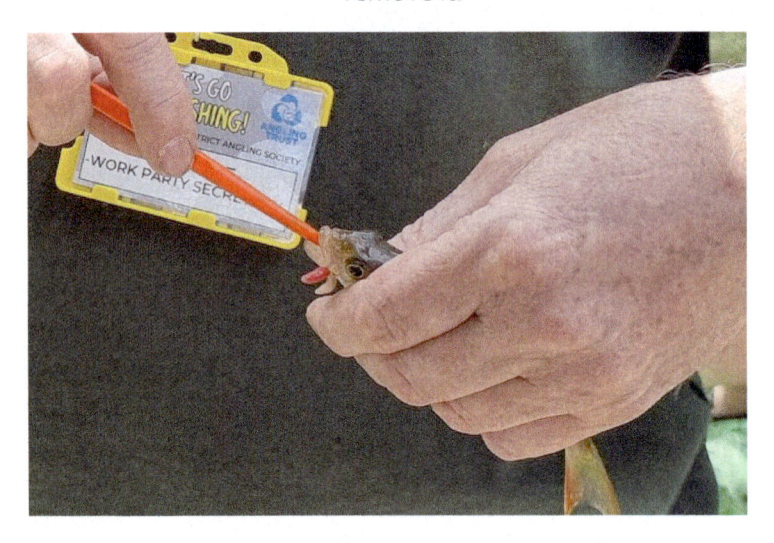

If the fish is deeply hooked and the hook can't be removed using a disgorger, very carefully try forceps. Otherwise, it is better to ask for help or cut the line as close to the hook as possible.

Fish Safety Tip! Always hold fish close to the ground when admiring or taking photo opportunities, the fish may escape your grasp and it may injure the fish. Also, keep the unhooking mats wet, more so when temperatures increase around summertime.

Returning fish to the water

Never throw a fish back into the water. Always get close to the water's edge to release a fish and let the fish swim away. If you catch a large fish, especially Barbel, it may have tired itself out while you were trying to land it. In this case, keep it in the landing net and hold the fish in the water facing the current until it is ready to swim away. Moving the fish backwards and forwards sometimes aids its recovery. If you wish to take photos of fish that you catch, please make sure all your equipment is set up ready. It is always best to have it setup correctly and well-rehearsed, this saves time, time which the fish do not have being out of the water. Keep the fish in the landing net until you are ready, if you want to weigh your fish then pop them back into the water until you are ready to do so. Try not to do both at once, fish cannot survive out of the water for very long. Splashing them with water is not good enough either, as the water needs to pass through the gills to have the oxygen filtered properly for them to breath. To work out how long you can keep a fish out of the water, it is always good practice to hold your own breath, if you start to struggle then the fish needs to go back.

Fish Facts

A guide to the anatomy of a fish

External anatomy

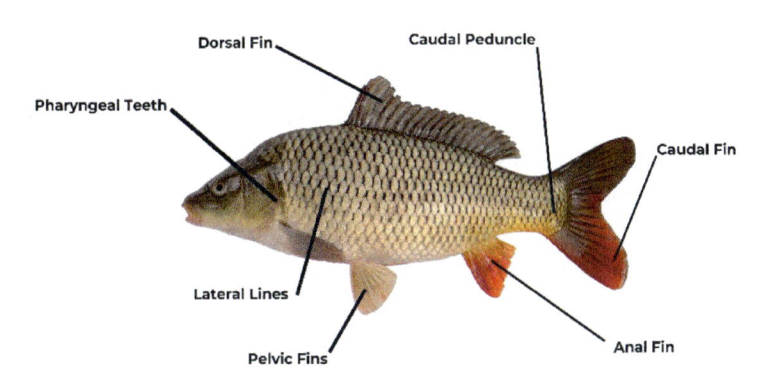

Fish diagram with labels: Dorsal Fin, Caudal Peduncle, Pharyngeal Teeth, Caudal Fin, Lateral Lines, Pelvic Fins, Anal Fin

Dorsal Fins

Looking at the external features of a fish first, each of the fins are designed for a specific task. The dorsal fin, for example, increase the lateral area of the fish. This helps to make it stable in the water when it is swimming albeit with slightly increased drag. Some species that have a long, continuous dorsal fin can ripple it all the way down - just enough to give a slight movement either forwards or backwards. On other species, like the European Bass (Dicentrarchus labrax) some of the dorsal fin rays are hard and sharp, a deterrent against predators, while in other species, like the lesser or greater weever fish, this defensive feature is taken even further with the addition of venomous spines that can inflict a painful injury.

Pelvic Fins

At the front of the lower body, there are two fins called the pelvic fins. These are there to help the fish change depth - either upwards or downwards - but also help it to make sudden stops or sharp turns. In some species, like Gobies (Pomatoschistus microps) these fins fuse together to make a sucker that the fish can use to cling to the rocks.

Operculum (Gill Cover)

The gill covers of fish, the operculum, cover and protect the gills whilst simultaneously allowing them to function. Other parts of the fish that are often referred to are the maxilla - the upper jaw - and the maxillary, which is a plate covering the hinge where the upper and lower jaws meet at the side of the head. Some fish, like Sharks and Flounders (Platichthys flesus) have spiracles, openings set behind the eyes where they can breathe in oxygenated water without the use of their gills. In some cases, this helps them to rest on the bottom without swimming while in others, like Flounders, they are believed to help increase the fish's olfactory ability - their sense of smell.

Pectoral Fins

Pectoral fins are often tucked tightly to the sides of the fish, especially when swimming at speed, but they can be flared to give lift, a feature that helps Sharks swim near the surface and which has been exaggerated even more in flying fish to propel them above the waves. On some species, like Angler Fish (Lophius piscatorius) the pectoral fins help them to 'walk' along the bottom, a stealthy strategy to help them change their position of ambush without giving themselves away!

Pharyngeal Teeth

Some species also have a second set of jaws and teeth in their throats, referred to as pharyngeal teeth. Species like Cyprinids, members of the Carp family, lack teeth in the oral cavity but do have a set of well-developed jaws and pharyngeal teeth in the gill arches where they can crush food items and help to pass them along to the stomach. In some fish, they are at the top and the bottom and in others, like most Cyprinids, they are at the sides.

Caudal Fin and Caudal Peduncle

Most of the propulsion for a fish comes from the tail, known as the caudal fin, which is often divided into upper and lower lobes. It attaches to the peduncle, often referred to as the caudal peduncle, which is the tapered area behind the dorsal and the anal fins.

Fast swimming fish, like Mackerel (Scomber scombrus) have narrow, highly tapered peduncles to which finlets, sometimes called adipose tufts, are attached to help them swim effectively at speed. Ambush predators, like Bass, have much wider peduncles to give them the short burst of speed necessary to rush from their hiding places and intercept their prey.

Anal Fin

The anal fin's function is to help keep the fish stable. This is usually found on the lower half of the body, just in front of the tail. Some species, like Catfish (Silurus glanis) and Salmon (Salmo salar) have a top, soft, fleshy fin set above it which is called an adipose fin. Scientists are not exactly sure what this fin does though some believe that it helps the fish respond to touch, sound, and changes in pressure. After suffering the loss of an adipose fin, fish have been observed beating their tails eight percent faster than they did before.

Lateral Lines

The lateral line, also called the lateral line organ (LLO), is a system of sensory organs found in fish, used to detect movement, vibration, and pressure gradients in the surrounding water. The sensory ability is achieved via modified epithelial cells, known as hair cells, which respond to displacement caused by motion and transduce these signals into electrical impulses via excitatory synapses. Lateral lines serve an important role in schooling behaviour, predation, and orientation.

Internal Anatomy

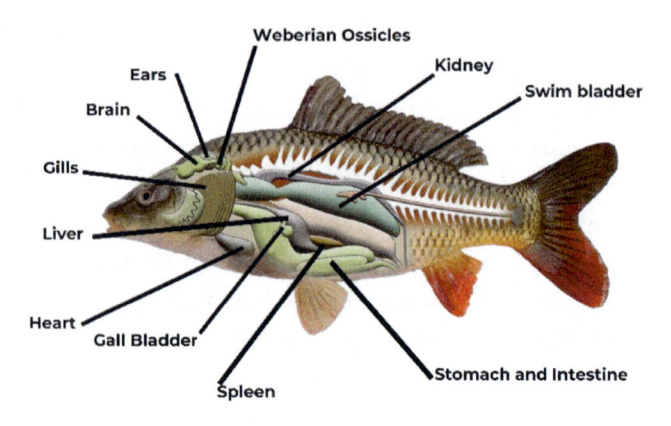

Gills

Gills of fish are for breathing. The gills sit behind the gill cover and, in a healthy fish, appear a bright red colour. The gills are extremely efficient at extracting oxygen from water allowing the fish to function normally. They can extract over 80% of the oxygen in the water passing over them (average person is around 4%). This efficiency comes at a price as the gills are very fragile, so the gill cover protects them from damage. Rough handling can easily damage them so anglers should try and avoid touching or handling a fish around the gills. The oxygen the fish extracts is used to 'burn' the food it has digested to provide the energy to survive.

Swim bladder

This organ stores gas inside the fish. Its main function is to counterbalance the weight of the rest of the fish's body. This means the fish does not have to swim to stay in the water column. It effectively makes the fish neutrally buoyant. This means the fins can be used to control position with slow precise movement rather than constantly having to work to keep itself off the bottom.

Weberian Ossicles

These are found only in the Carp-like fish. They are bone extensions of the spine and connect the swim bladder to the fish's ears. This connection means that the fish can hear a much wider range of sound frequencies. Fish like Perch and Pike do not have these and so have less effective hearing.

Kidney

A fish's two kidneys are merged into one and sit right under the spine. The kidney's main function is to act as a filter and is well developed in all freshwater fish. It filters the blood and allows the fish to get rid of all the water that leaks into its body across the gills and through the intestine. The rest of the outside skin of the fish is watertight unless it gets damaged. If the kidney gets damaged by disease or pollution, the fish retains water and will bloat up because it cannot effectively get rid of the water.

Spleen

A dark red organ usually located around the middle of the fish. This organ makes and stores blood and helps to fight off infections.

Brain

Fish brains are not massive but perfectly functional for what the fish needs. They are particularly well developed for processing sensory information such as vision, smell, and sounds.

Stomach and Intestine

Predatory fish have stomachs to process the ingested prey. Fish like Carp and Roach do not have a true stomach and just have a long intestine. This is because they feed more frequently than predators and their natural food often comes in smaller bits. This means they do not need a stomach to start the digestion process. Food travels down the gut and is soaked with digestive chemicals to break it down. It is then absorbed by the intestine and transported by blood to the liver or is stored for later use.

Ears

The ears of fish are internal with no connection to the outside world. The reason for this is simply that they do not need to. Sound travels much better in water compared to air so the sound easily passes into the fish where their ears can detect it. Fish hear much lower pitch sounds than people but are not as good at hearing high pitched sounds. You should remember this when you are trampling about on the bank or banging in bank sticks.

Gall Bladder

This produces bile which is secreted into the intestine to neutralise acid from the stomach and helps digest fats in food. It is usually bright yellow or green depending on the colour of the bile it produces.

Heart

This is a blood pump, just like in people. In fish, blood leaves the heart and goes directly to the gills. So, when the blood arrives at the gills it is at high pressure and flowing fast. This helps to make the gills efficient in carrying oxygen and food, as well as transporting waste chemicals. The blood then travels away from the gills carrying oxygen to other body organs. However, it also means that if the gills are damaged the blood loss is quite rapid – so avoid handling fish near the gills. The heart sits under the gills usually in the V-shape formed between the two gill covers. This location ensures the heart does not have to pump blood far to get to the gills.

Liver

The liver of most of our coarse fish is usually quite big and combines the liver and pancreas together. This organ regulates and processes the digested food. It can also break down harmful chemicals. In coarse fish it is usually connected closely with the intestine. If it gets damaged it means the fish cannot process food properly and they can waste away and die. In coarse fish fed on trout pellets it can also get quite fatty. Yet however, there is no real evidence that this does the fish any harm.

Bait basics

A beginners guide to using bait

What is fishing bait?

Fishing bait is the most important thing you need to catch a fish. It is the very thing that we use to lure the fish in, to attract them to the swim and to feed them. Bait has evolved other the centuries, so much so that it can now be categorised into groups.

- Live baits
- Boilies
- Pellets
- Groundbait
- Particle feed
- Imitation bait
- Household foods
- Artificial Lures

There is so much choice of bait filling the shelves in tackle shops, even supermarkets hold a quarry of baits to catch fish. Each bait can catch several types of species, some of which most fish will eat, but other baits like boilies, are designed to target specific species.

What is a live bait?

These are baits that are living, such as worms or maggots, but can also be small fish that are attached to a rig to catch the bigger predatory fish like Pike. These fish can be used either alive or dead.

- Maggot (Also Pinkie and Squatt)
- Worm – Lob, Dendrobaena, Brandling,
- Live/Dead fish baits – Silver fish like Roach, Bream, and Rudd

What is a maggot?

Maggots are the larvae stage of a fly, it is the stage between the egg and the chrysalis (also known as 'caster'). There are three types of maggots that anglers use, and they are different sizes.

- Squatt - the larvae of the small House fly
- Pinkie - the larvae of the Greenbottle fly
- Maggot - the larvae of the European Bluebottle fly

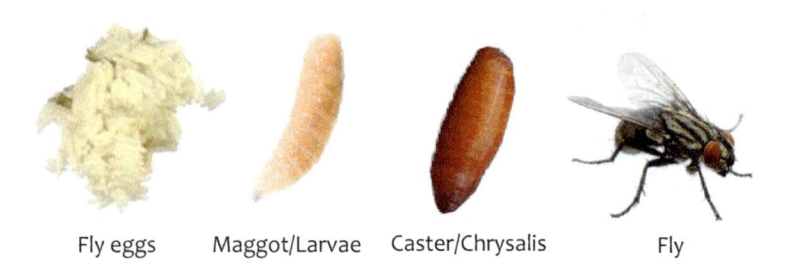

Fly eggs   Maggot/Larvae   Caster/Chrysalis   Fly

The usual colour of a maggot is a creamy white, but you can also buy them in a myriad of colours. Most popular is red, but they are available in bronze, green, fluoro pink and even blue. The different colours help to trick the fish into thinking they are different bugs such as caterpillars that have fallen from trees or of bug larvae. As with all living things, maggots do not stay fresh for long if not kept properly. Storing maggots isn't that difficult but does require a few things to keep them for longer and between session.

The best place to keep maggots is in a fridge. And if bought fresh, can last up to 2 weeks. The cold slows their metabolism down and prevents them from changing into casters. Always keep the lid on tight to prevent any damp maggots from escaping inside the fridge. If you cannot keep them in a fridge, then a cold dark place is best. To keep maggots for longer, they need to be looked after. This is where something called a 'riddle' comes in to play.

How to riddle maggots

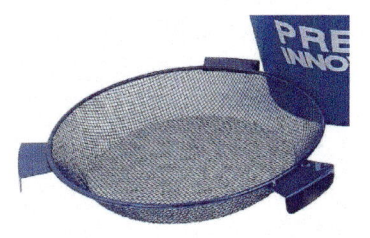

It is best to riddle maggots at least once a day to remove any dead ones (also known as skins) and any maggots that have turned to casters (these can be collected and frozen – they make very good loose feed as well as hook bait). You will need a clean and dry tray, pour your maggots onto the riddle, and allow them to wriggle through of their own accord. All the debris and dead ones will be left on the riddle – just feed those to your garden birds. Place these live ones into your bait box along with some maize dust to keep them dry and fresh.

What is a bait box?

These are tubs for storing bait and have lids that seal tight, this is to keep live baits such as maggots from escaping. The lids have holes in to allow fresh air to reach the maggots, to not only keep them alive, but also helps reduce condensation from forming inside. It is always best to only half-fill a bait box to prevent the maggots from sweating as they wriggle amongst each other.

How to hook a maggot

Grip the maggot with a slight pinch with 2 fingers, in your weaker hand. For example, if you are right-handed, hold the maggot with left hand. Ensure the blunt end of the maggot is exposed, this is identifiable by a slight ridge across the end and two dots. This is the rear end to the maggot, the pointed/tapered tip is the head area, where the mouth is.

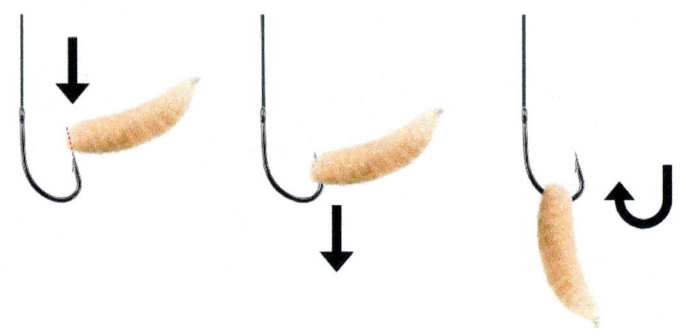

Guide the point of the hook through the raised area, and gently push it around the bend of the hook. If you are using small hooks, ush the maggot around to the flat of the hook shank.

If using more than one maggot on a hook that is barbless, hook the second maggot through tip of the pointy end.

This helps to stop them wriggling off the hook when in the water. If the maggot bursts, it is always best practice to pull it off, discard it and start again.

What are worms?

Worms are universal in distribution, occurring in the sea water, freshwater, and terrestrial habitats like the soil. Some types of worms are parasitic, others are free-living.

Fishing worms are the free-living variety and are also important soil conditioners.

The most common worm used for fishing is the Dendrobaena worm closely followed by the Lob worm depending on what type of fish you are trying to attract.

There is also the brandling, a red earthworm with rings of a brighter colour, typically found in manure, and used as bait by anglers although not as popular.

Worms a mostly used as a hook bait but are also great as loose feed or in groundbait. In much the same way as the maggot, but they tend to be chopped up and mixed in.

How to hook a worm

It is always best to hook a worm through the banded area known as the 'saddle', as this is the toughest bit on the worm.

Make sure the hook size isn't too small for the worm you are using, you want the point to be clearly visible. Some anglers like to cut off the end of the worm, as this can help attract fish using the scent being released from the worm as it wriggles in the water.

How to use Dendrobaena worms

Dendrobaena are used in both natural and commercial venues, to attract Tench, Chub, Perch, Roach, and Carp. Most anglers will hook a Dendrobaena straight on the hook. Some will chop them up and mix them into ground baits to create a chopped worm mix. This will then either be balled in or used in method feeders.

How to use Lob Worms

Lob worms are another great live bait for fishing. These are more favoured on natural fishing venues like rivers and old estate lakes/ponds and are great for attracting large Perch, Chub, Bream, Eels, Tench, Pike and even Catfish.

What are live/dead fish baits?

Live or dead fish baits can be used in a variety of methods, either by being held under a large float or ledgered on the bottom. Fishing with live bait is a method used primarily for predatory fish, so they will not work when using them to catch something like a Bream. Any coarse fish can prove successful in catching a predatory fish. Gudgeon are small but are favoured by many predator anglers. The most commonly used bait is likely to be a Roach or skimmer Bream. This is probably due to their bright, shiny flanks and the fact they can be caught in most waters. But Dead baits can also be sea fish such as Mackerel, Shad, Whiting, or small chunks of larger species.

Live baiting is quite a contentious issue, so it is up to you to decide whether to use the method or not. Although, it is very important to note that the controlling club on the fishery you are at will also have rules about live baiting. If it's allowed at the fishery, you'll only be allowed to use baits caught from the fishery. This is to stop disease being introduced to the fishery from another water.

How to hook a live/dead fish bait

The simplest way is to use a large hook and hook it through the lip, although other methods use treble hooks. Most often, these rigs are set up with wire traces, this is similar to a hook length but is wire instead of fishing line and helps prevent the fish from biting through the line with their sharp teeth.

What is a boilie?

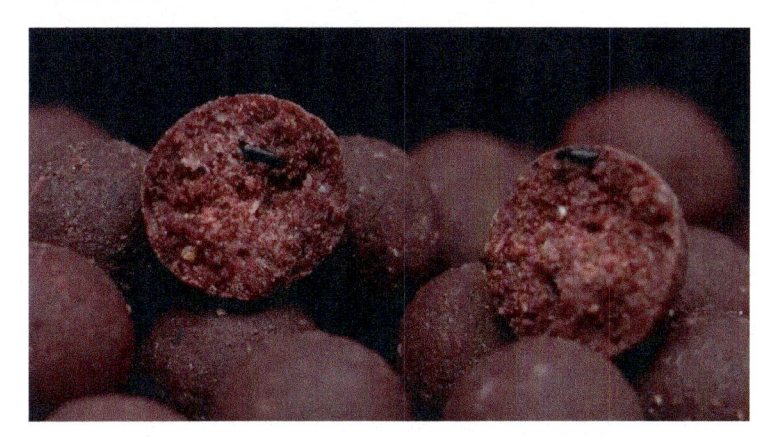

Boilies are a type of fishing bait that is made from a paste, this is then rolled, formed, and then boiled (hence the name). They usually consist of base mixes of fishmeal, milk proteins, bird foods, semolina, and soya flour. This is mixed together using egg as a binding agent. The mixture is boiled for a few minutes to form round baits with hardened outer coatings, and these will last in the water. Additional flavourings and other forms of aromatic attractants are also in the mixture to increase scent and flavour. The round shape allows the baits to be catapulted accurately when fishing at distant waters and help to give a better presentation when hair rigged on the hook. Some boilies have added buoyant product which makes them either slightly lift off the lakebed, known as a 'wafter' or fully buoyant, which is known as a 'pop up'.

How to use a boilie

There are many ways to attach a boilie to a hook, the simplest method is something called a hair rig. This is where you tie a knotless knot (See *'knot knowledge' section*) and use a baiting needle.

With the baiting needle (if it has a latch, ensure this is folded back), pierce it through the middle of the boilie, and then push it through until it comes out the other side.

Hook the loop on the end (if you have latch, this is where you will need to close it).

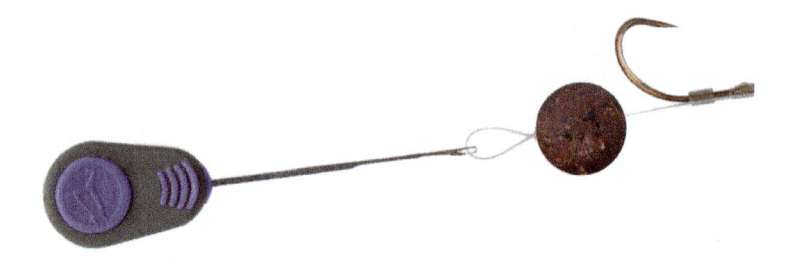

Whilst holding the needle, push the boilie onto the hair.

You then remove the needle from the loop and place a boilie stop into the loop and pull the boilie tight to the stop. This traps the boilie in between the hook and the stop.

Other methods of attaching a boilie

The number of ways in which you can attach a boilie is vast and always an evolving thing. One of the most well-known is the 'Ronnie rig', and this is essentially a low-lying pop-up rig, enabling the boilie to subtly sit up just off the lakebed making it ideal for when there is not too much weed or debris. The boilie is attached with bait floss, this is thread through the micro swivel and the boilie is attached using a baiting needle. Once pulled through, the ends of the floss are trimmed and melted with a lighter.

The Ronnie rig

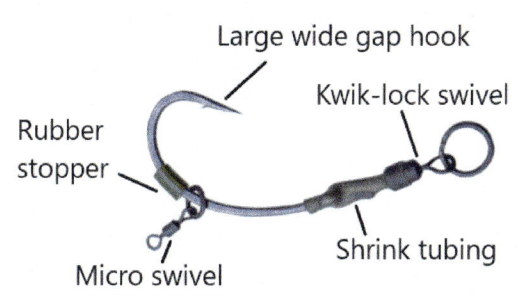

Other methods involve using bait screws, these attach to the hook in the same fashion as the micro swivel on the Ronnie rig. These offer a very simple way to attach bait and quickly change it if needed.

Aside from the ways in which we can attach a boilie, there are also ways in which we can loose feed them. The common use of PVA string or mesh has some huge advantages, being that it melts in water. This allows the angler to attach several matching baits to the hook, once melted they give a good presentation of the bait around the intended hook bait.

There are many products out there that use PVA, and all have their uses (Not just for carp fishing!).

What is a pellet?

Pellets are a great addition to any coarse and match bait. Pellets are probably the second favourite option after groundbait. Pellets come in various shapes, colours, and sizes. The main types of pellets are feed pellets, hook pellets and expanding pellets (these expand when soaked). There are so many flavours to choose from, tackle shops have isle dedicated to them. Similar to groundbait, pellets are flavoured in a similar way; you can get sweet and sticky pellets which are ideal for using in method feeders, and fishmeal pellets. Fishmeal pellets tend to be more readily available and therefore cheaper to buy; many are used in commercial fisheries for carp as this is what the carp were farmed on originally.

Hook pellets come in various forms, they can be small pre-drilled pellets for hair rigging, or soft hooker pellets.

These pellets tend to be soaked in liquid attractants to help bring in the fish. You can always add your own a liquid attractant to your pellets giving you that extra edge in matches on commercials.

The most popular methods of fishing with pellets are pellet waggler and feeder fishing. The bait is either hair rigged to the hook or attached using a pellet band (this can be either be used tied to a hair or banding the bait with the shank of the hook).

When used in feeder fishing, the pellets are soaked for a short period to allow them to form easily on the feeder, these then loosen when they are sitting on the lakebed.

What is groundbait?

Groundbait is simply a way of attracting fish to your swim. It can vary as to what ingredients are in it, but its main job is to give you pulling power, scented groundbait has great pulling power to attract fish into your swim. It will give fish confidence to feed in your area and keeps them in the area to improve your chances of catching more than one. It can also help to get your feed down to the bottom of the bed to make it easier to fish. i.e., as a binder, it will hold your pellets, maggots and worms and live bait and take it to the bottom of the bed. It will then break down and release the feed in a tight spot.

The simplest groundbait is white crumb or punch crumb, this is simply dried breadcrumb, milled into a powder. Ideal for winter fishing for Roach and skimmers. The second most popular groundbaits are fishmeal groundbaits, basically dried out fish ground up to a very fine powder, perfect for Carp, Tench, and Bream.

Another type of groundbait is made using crushed up biscuits, a lot of groundbaits from the continent are made up of this and tend to be much sweeter and blended with hemp, molasses, and particles. Biscuits are also ideal for binding groundbaits. Bream love this type of groundbait and Roach love chocolate flavoured groundbait. You can also get active or inactive groundbaits.

Active groundbaits will fall down to the bottom and fizz, these tend to have hemp particles in to help create this frenzied effect.

Inactive or inert groundbaits tend to be more like your method mixes which will stick together in one lump. Some particles will still fall out of the inactive groundbait to attract fish. Fish like Chub and Barbel prefer active groundbaits in rivers and lakes, Carp, Bream, and Tench prefer inactive groundbait, they will smell the groundbait on the lakebed and their movement will swirl up the water and groundbait creating clouds that will in turn attract more fish.

There are so many types of groundbait available, different colours, different ingredients and all aimed at a group of species or various methods of fishing. It is always a very good thing to talk to your local tackle shop, as they can often tell you what is working best at that current time and for what species of fish you are targeting.

How to use groundbait

There are a couple of ways we can use groundbait to draw fish into the swim. The most popular method (mainly used in float fishing) is to squeeze it into balls and throw it in or catapult it into the swim. Another method is to use an open end/groundbait feeder, fill it up and cast it out.

Some anglers use groundbait when feeder fishing, but others sometimes use a feeder setup just to get groundbait on the bottom in their swim, as it provides a far more accurate presentation of attractant. The feeder method is also beneficial as you can feed the swim in smaller amounts, as when balling it in you can sometimes overfeed the area and spook fish.

How to prepare groundbait

Regardless as to whether you choose a shop bought mixed groundbait or you have your own recipe, the preparation is still roughly the same. There are different ways to prepare groundbait, as each method has its uses. A stickier mix is more ideal for a deeper water or for long range distribution, whilst a fluffier mix is better for quick release. Small nuggets of sloppy ground bait can send particles swirling down the current at some distance and this will attract the interest of large Roach and Chub.

You will need a large mixing bowl or bucket, there are bowls sold in shops that are perfect for the job, but a large round bowl of any sorts will still work. A riddle of some form is needed to remove formed lumps and produce a much finer finish. A container for water will be needed to add to the mixture and some form of atomising spray bottle filled with water (this is helpful to stop it from drying out over a long session).

Top tip! You can always add more water, but you can't take it out! so add water in small amounts each time until you get the results you desire (if you are adding attractants, then take this into account).

To start, add the bait to your bowl or bucket and then gradually add water.

You will usually be looking for the consistency of wet sand or something similar to how cookie dough feels.

Imagine wet sand that you could build a sandcastle with, not too sloppy but enough to form shapes.

Mix vigorously so that all of the particles can absorb the moisture, use your hands.

You can also add loose feed into this mix, more commonly to match the hook bait. Maggots, casters, sweetcorn, and hemp are popular loose feeds but there are many to choose from.

At this stage you may also wish to include attractants in your mixture, remember to mix thoroughly as well as ensuring what you add isn't going to make it too wet.

Leave this for around 10-15 minutes, then pour it through a riddle (this stage isn't essential but can help with the groundbait breaking down quicker). By experimenting with your mixes and attractants and the way you feed them, you will discover what works best for you, your target fish, and your chosen venue.

What is particle feed?

Particle feed is the term used to describe feed such as seeds, nuts or pulses used within coarse fishing. It is often added to groundbait but has become very popular with specimen fishing for species such as Carp.

What types of particle feed are there?

There are many particle baits to use, here are just a few that are the most popular.

- Hemp
- Tares
- Millet
- Maize
- Nuts – Tiger nuts, peanuts etc.
- Bird seed – various mixes (pigeon conditioner is popular)
- Beans – Black eyed, butter, soy, and kidney beans

How to prepare particle feed

Most particle feed can be bought in tackle shops pre-prepared ready for use, but some anglers like to buy in bulk to save costs. This means they often have to prepare it themselves.

Fish safety tip! Undercooked particle baits can kill fish, so make sure it is cooked and prepared correctly.

Most particles, pulses and seeds need to be soaked and / or boiled and simmered before they are safe for the fish to eat or to be used as a loose feed. Some particles can swell up to three times their original size as they are soaked and take in water. Some particles such as hemp and tiger nuts have a strong natural flavour and scent, so may not need any flavouring added. As with all flavouring of baits it is a personal choice and help to give that added edge. It is always best to add any flavourings and attractants to the soaking mix, as this gives it more time to soak into the particles.

How long do particles take to prepare?

Particle baits should be soaked for 12-24 hours, then boiled and simmered for 20 to 30 minutes. In the case of Nuts (Peanuts, Tiger nuts etc) it is recommended to soak them for 36-48 hours before boiling and simmering for 20 minutes. Particles that are prepared and cooked thoroughly are soft throughout. While soaking any flavours or additives can be added. There is no one method for all, but it is always best to overcook than to under cook them.

How to use particle baits

Particles can be used as in groundbait, as a loose feed or hook bait. As a hook bait use straight on the hook or on a hair rig. Smaller particles can be hooked such as hemp, maize, and beans. Other particles that are larger, like tiger nuts, are best used with a hair rig method.

Some anglers use particles in PVA bags or mesh, these can then be made up and added to the rig, cast out to the spot and the bait is then released directly with the hook bait and gives good presentation of bait and loose feed. *(See 'Rigs & techniques' section)*

Particles can also be added to spod/spomb mix, this is where something called a 'spod' or a 'spomb' is tethered to a specific rod and reel setup. It is then filled with particles and other loose feeds and cast out to the spot required. This allows larger amounts of bait delivered in one cast, mostly used specimen fishing for species such as Carp.

What is imitation bait?

Imitation bait is basically a fake bait used to capture fish. This can be a basic imitation bait such as maggot or caster to an artificial bread.

How to use imitation bait

With imitation bait, the main reason they have become popular is because they are trying to target specific species such as Carp or Barbel and do not want the bait being chewed up by smaller silver fish. Other reasons include using imitation baits that are buoyant, that make it easier to present a popped-up bait off the bottom where the fish can easily see it. There is also the reason that imitation baits can't be knocked off the hook or break down in the water with baits such as bread.

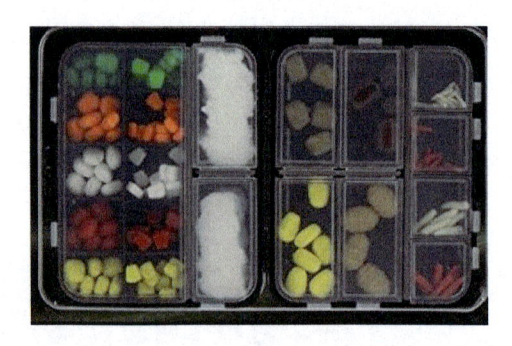

Imitation bait is used in place of most hook baits, either on the hook or hair rigged. They can even to be added after a boilie or pellet on a hair rig to help add a better attractive look. They can be boosted with attractants and can be reused time and time again.

What household foods can be used for fishing?

There are so many foods that we keep in our kitchens that can be used as bait. The most popular foods are bread, sweetcorn, and luncheon meat. These baits will catch most species of coarse fish, if used in the right way. The choice is staggering and too much to put in this book, so here are a few of the most popular food items used as bait and how to use them.

Sweetcorn

This is a cheap form of bait which requires little preparation. It is sweet in taste and bright in colour and is often proven to be irresistible to a variety of fish including Carp, Tench, Bream, and Roach. Sweetcorn can also easily be coloured or flavoured to make it more attractive to fish. Always remember to empty the tin into a resealable tub, this helps reduce the chances of littering.

How to hook Sweetcorn

Sweetcorn can be put straight on the hook or hair rigged (same method as a boilie). There are a few ways to hook the Sweetcorn, although match anglers swear by hooking it through the top. Sweetcorn can be used as a single bait or with a few on the hook or hair.

Luncheon meat

Most brands of luncheon meat or 'spam' will work. It is best to prepare this the day before fishing by cutting it into cubes, this will allow the meat to dry out a little, or it will be far too moist to use. Luncheon meat is a prolific bait to use for bigger species of fish such as Barbel and Chub, but you will need to use large chunks of it.

You could try other types of meat as well, provided you can get it to stay on the hook, and dog food has even been known to bag a decent fish. Other meats can be sections of Peperami, chorizo, and other dry cured meats.

How to use luncheon meat

The same as sweetcorn, this can be used either hair rigged (same as boilies) or on the hook (although with bigger chunks, the hook will need to be buried inside).

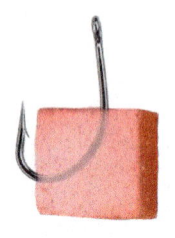

Bread

Bread can be used as a hook bait in many different ways and more often than not it can help to attract a better stamp of fish. It can be crumbed up to create groundbait or loose feed, but also as a versatile hook bait.

How to use bread

Fold over the hook

Pinch around hook shank

It can be used in flake form by just pulling a small piece (around the size of a thumb print), placing the hook in the middle, and pinching the bread around the hook's shank.

Another method is to use a small crust of bread which will float on the surface and provide a perfect floating bait to tempt fish such as Carp and Chub in the warmer months.

You can also use a bread punch, which is used to punch out small pieces of bread, a similar size to a hole punch (but there are various sizes). These punched out pieces of bread can be placed on a small hook, although some anglers also like to put 2 or 3 of them on a hair rig.

UK Fish Species

A comprehensive guide to freshwater fish

Barbel

Barbus barbus
Cyprinidae Family

Average weight

In the UK, an average Barbel grows to 20-35" (0.5-0.9m) in length and weighs between 6-16 lbs (2.6-7.25kg).

Description

The Barbel is light brown in colour with slight yellowing of sides and a whitish underbody. The body of the barbel is long and powerfully slender with small scales, 55 to 65 scales along the lateral line and give the appearance of the fish being scale-less. The head of the barbel is tapered and its eyes which are small are set high on the sides of the head The barbel is recognised by its under slung mouth with very thick lips and two short barbules on the top lip and two longer barbules at the corner of its mouth. These barbules have taste, touch cells, and help the fish to locate food on the riverbed.

Habitat

The Barbel are bottom feeders and like to root around, feeding in the gravel bottom of fast flowing rivers. A powerful fish with a body shape perfect for living in fast flowing waters barbel are regarded as the hardest fighting coarse fish in the river. Although barbel are caught all year round they are more of a summer and autumn fish. During the summer months barbel can be found in weir pools and the faster stretches of water, so look for creases in the waters flow. In weir pools follow the froth and bubbles, as this tends to tell you the flow characteristics. During the autumn and winter months the fish favour the deeper more slower waters, so slacks and eddies are the best places to start.

Swim choice

On smaller rivers in low water conditions when it is a little slower or when normal water conditions are frequent, you will find the Barbel anywhere throughout the stretch. This can be in the slower deep pools or near the fast shallow glides and anywhere in-between. However, you will sometimes find that Barbel prefers to be close to some form of cover, be that weed, rafts, submerged snags, or overhanging trees. This is often to avoid predation from large birds, but also sometimes is a resting spot from the faster currents when food sources are lower.

Baits and loose feeds

The most popular hook baits for catching Barbel

- Luncheon meat
- Pellets (Halibut/Garlic/Krill/Spicy Meat)
- Small boilies (10-12mm)
- Maggots
- Casters
- Cheese paste and cheese cubes
- Dendrobaena worms, red worm, Brandlings and Lob worms
- Bread, either crust, flake or paste
- Sausage, such as Peperami
- Sweetcorn
- Bread
- Cheese paste

The most popular loose feeds for catching Barbel

- Hemp – The No1 Barbel feed
- Groundbait – Base flavours of Fishmeal/Meat/Garlic
- Castors and Maggots
- Chopped worm
- Sweetcorn
- Breadcrumb

Methods

The ledger or feeder are considered the best methods for catching Barbel, but they can even be caught using float fishing methods. The Barbel inhabits strong, fast flowing waters, so a strong rod (1lb t/c minimum) is needed. A reel, spooled with a minimum of 6lb line, should ideally be used (stronger if in very snaggy areas - around 10-12lb). Hook sizes between 12 and 8 are ideal, a minimalist approach is considered the best practice. Hook lengths need to be longer than normal, so anything from 1 ft to 5 ft dependant on flow and how clear the water is.

The Barbel is cautious when feeding, more so in an area that is fished frequently. When using hair rigged baits, longer hairs help to avoid the greedy Chub and help with the wary Barbel.

Fish safety tip! When a Barbel is hooked, it will NOT give up easily and it will fight until it is exhausted. Try to land and unhook the fish quickly. When landed and unhooked, hold the barbel in the flowing water facing upstream until it is ready to swim away. This can take a couple of minutes to 15 minutes or longer. A landing net over 30" is ideal and using a decent sized unhooking mat is considered good practice.

Top tip! Ideal times to find active barbel are early in the morning and a couple of hours before or after dusk. The Barbel requires water temperatures of at least 7°C to feed properly and are caught throughout summer and autumn.

Bleak

Alburnus alburnas
Cyprinidae Family

Average weight

The average size of the common Bleak is 12-15 cm. The maximum size is 20 cm, and the weight is up to 50 grams. It matures sexually in the third year of its life at a length of 7-8 cm.

Description

It is a slender fish with an elongated and flat sided body. It has a pointed head with large eyes and a small mouth that is turned upwards. Colouration of the Bleak is a shiny silvery colour. The body is covered with large scales, the back and flanks are silvery blue/green, merging into silver down the sides to a white belly. The lateral line is complete, and the fins are pointed and colourless with a long anal fin concave at the edge and forked tail.

Habitat

Bleak can be found in most streams, lakes and the slower moving rivers but prefers open waters. It is a shoal fish and often found in quite large shoals, living, and feeding in the upper layers of the water

Swim choice

On smaller rivers and streams, the Bleak can be found in shoals, in the well covered parts of the water. However, in larger bodies of water, such as lakes, they tend to be in larger groups and on the top part of the water column.

Baits and loose feeds

The most popular hook baits for catching Bleak

- Maggot
- Pinkies
- Caster
- Small red worm
- Brandling
- Pieces of worm
- Small pieces of bread, and bread punch

The most popular loose feeds for catching Bleak

- Hemp
- Groundbait – Base flavours of Fishmeal/Sweet/Cereal
- Castors and Maggots
- Chopped worm
- Breadcrumb

Methods

Bleak can be caught on light float tackle. Using a float rod or whip, place most of the shot under the float so that the bait falls through the water slowly. Using maggot as bait, put 1 or 2 on a size 16 or 18 hook. With a shoal of Bleak nearby, you will find that bites come fast and furious, even catching on maggot skins. A few loose fed maggots will keep them interested.

Fish safety tip! Due to these fish having very small mouths, try not to allow the bites to over develop as unhooking them can be fatal, as they swallow the hook and bait too deeply. Ensure you have a small hook disgorger to hand. When handling the fish be aware that the scales are loose and very easily dislodged.

Top tip! The Bleak is not usually targeted by the general angler but because they swim in large shoals and are easy to catch the match angler can soon whip up a big weight. Like the Gudgeon, the Bleak has saved the day for many a match angler from blanking.

Bream – Common (Bronze)

Abramis braba
Cyprinidae Family

Average weight

An average common Bream will be 12" - 14". The Bream grows up to 19lb+ and a fish over 4lb considered a good fish.

Description

Adults are deep bodied and bronze in colour with darker, sometimes black fins. The Bream has a deep laterally compressed body with a prominent covering of protective slime. It has a long anal fin compared with the dorsal fin, a forked tail and a small head and mouth with a protruding upper jaw. Young Bream up to approximately 8oz. are known as 'skimmers' and are silver in colour but turn a darker bronze colour as they mature. Often the small Bream is mistaken for the Silver Bream (Abramis bjoerkna).

Habitat

Bream are bottom feeders, travelling in shoals, rooting around and feeding in the soft bottom of ponds, lakes, and the lower reaches of rivers.

Swim choice

Bream will always favour the cover of weed beds, lilies, and tree cover. They tend to prefer areas that give them shade from the sun and sanctuary from predators, whilst also providing a food source in the shape of insects and snails. Large catches have resulted from laying down a carpet of groundbait which holds the shoal in the area, but often too much groundbait can spook the swim.

Baits and loose feeds

The most popular hook baits for catching Bream

- Dendrobaena worms, lob worms, small red worm, and brandlings
- Bloodworm
- Bread (either punch, flake or paste)
- Casters
- Maggots
- Pinkies
- Sweetcorn
- Boilies (sweet, but any carp flavour will work)
- Pellets (same as the boilies)

The most popular loose feeds for catching Bream

- Hemp
- Groundbait – Base flavours of Continental/Sweet/Fishmeal/Cereal
- Brown crumb
- Sweetcorn
- Casters
- Chopped worms
- Pellets
- Boilie crumb/flake

Methods

Various methods can catch Bream, including float, ledger, or feeder. The feeder, by far, is considered the best method.
Once a fish is hooked it needs to be pulled away from the shoal quickly otherwise the shoal will be spooked and will move on. When feeder fishing, use an open-ended feeder filled with a groundbait mix with some of your hook bait mixed in and a hook length of 18 - 24 ". When you cast in and the feeder has reached the bottom, wind up the slack in the line, and wind in a little more until there is a slight bend on your rod tip.

Float fishing for Bream is also a good technique on well stocked lakes or ponds. Fishing on the bottom with plenty of loose feed and groundbait to get them feeding confident, then small amounts with each cast.

Fish safety tip! The Bream is considered one of the slimiest of UK fish species (although there are worse!), often leaving a snotty residue when handling. This coating is essential for the Bream's protection against infections and scale damage, so do not use towels or gloves when handling. Worthwhile having a spare towel handy to clean up after a catch.

Top tip! Bream bites are noticeable when float fishing by the slow disappearance of the float or when ledger / feeder fishing by the steady pull round of your rod tip. The Bream is not known as a fighting fish and after a few 'nods' (tugs on the line as you reel in) come to the net with little resistance.

Bream – Silver

Abramis bjoerkna
Cyprinidae Family

Average weight

The Silver Bream, when living in large bodies of water has a maximum size of just 450g (1 lb) and when found in small ponds, they rarely go over 350g (12 oz).

Description

Silver Bream are not as widespread in the UK waters as the common Bronze Bream and very rarely are they specifically fished for. Silver Bream are smaller but are like a young common Bream and difficult to tell apart, often mistaken for a skimmer Bream or a hybrid. The silver Bream is a deep bodied fish with a dark olive-green back, silvery sides and white under belly. The fins are pale and may be tinged pinkish. They also have a small head with large round, protruding eyes with a yellowish cornea and black iris, this can also help distinguish it from the skimmer bream. Found in lakes, ponds, rivers, and canals but more often found in still waters.

Habitat

Silver Bream Found in lakes, ponds, rivers, and canals but more often found in still waters.

Swim choice

As with the common Bream, silver Bream will always favour the cover of weed beds, lilies, and tree cover. They tend to prefer areas that give them shade from the sun and sanctuary from predators, whilst also providing a food source in the shape of insects and snails. Better results come from laying down a carpet of groundbait which holds the shoal in the area, but often too much groundbait can spook the swim.

Baits and loose feeds

The most popular hook baits for catching Bream

- Dendrobaena worms, small red worm, and brandlings
- Bloodworm
- Bread (either punch, flake or paste)
- Casters
- Maggots
- Pinkies
- Sweetcorn
- Small Pellets

The most popular loose feeds for catching Bream

- Hemp
- Groundbait – Base flavours of Continental/Fishmeal
- Sweetcorn
- Casters
- Chopped worms
- Pellets

Methods

Fishing for silver Bream is like fishing for common Bream, although lighter tackle should be used. A setup with fine lines, small hooks, and small baits suitable for catching small fish such as roach is ideal.

Various methods are used to catch Silver Bream including float, ledger, or feeder.

Fish safety tip! The silver Bream is not considered to be as slimy as the common Bream, but the handling should remain the same process. This coating is essential for the silver Bream's protection against infections and scale damage, so do not use towels or gloves when handling. Worthwhile having a spare towel handy to clean up after a catch.

Top tip! Bream bites are noticeable when float fishing by the slow disappearance of the float or when ledger / feeder fishing by the steady pull round of your rod tip. The Bream is not known as a fighting fish and after a few 'nods' (tugs on the line as you reel in) come to the net with little resistance.

Carp – Common (King)

Cyprinus carpio
Cyprinidae Family

Average weight

Common, mirror and leather Carp are all particularly clever, hard fighting fish and in the UK have an average weight of 6-20 lbs (2.7-9 kg) and grow to an average length of 18-26"(45-65 cm). In the UK they can grow to weights over 40 lbs (18 kg) and a fish above 15 lb (6.8 kg) is very common and would be considered a good catch.

Description

There are many sub species of the common king Carp. The common Carp is a fully scaled and large bodied. The mirror Carp is scaled with large, uneven mirror like scales, and these have smooth bodies when there are no scales. The linear Carp is scale less except for a row of large scales that run along the lateral line on both sides. The leather Carp is smooth bodied, virtually unscaled except near dorsal fin. The ghost Carp is the same as the common Carp, but it is all white with two black eyes.

There are other variants of Carp, such as the grass Carp, which are like the common Carp but normally has a longer, thinner body. The koi Carp is more of an ornamental fish. Unlike the common Carp, it is colours can include orange, black, red, yellow, as well as combination of these colours. The F1 Carp are a crossbreed of the crucian and the common Carp and have 1 set of barbules. There is also the wild Carp, which are known to be the originally introduced variant to the England and Wales by monks in the early 1300's. Carp can be found in all waters but are predominantly fished for in still waters.

Habitat

Carp fishing is more prolific during the summer months, leading into autumn. During the colder months in winter and the beginning of spring, the fish become dormant. Carp will feed in winter if there is a prolonged mild. Carp feed any time of the day, but the best times to fish for them are early mornings during the summer months, late evenings and the first few hours of darkness.

The Carp develops well in lakes with heavy weed growth and lake beds that are very silty. All the carp sub species are omnivorous, and so in environments like this, they are surrounded by food. The natural diet of most Carp is very varied and includes plants, seeds, snails, insect larvae, worms, molluscs, and crustaceans.

Swim choice

Carp are often found close to the bank and cruise around the edge when feeding, particularly if the weather is warmer. In hot weather you will often see them on the surface, as they tend to move up the water column when the temperatures increase. Look for cloudy/disturbed areas where there are signs of feeding., sometimes bubbling at the surface or fish showing (jumping out the water) are good signs to.

In the colder months, the Carp move into the middle of the lake, where it is deeper and often are slow to feed.

Baits and loose feeds

The most popular hook baits for catching Carp

- Boilies
- Luncheon Meat
- Pellets
- Chum mixers or any other dog/cat biscuits (surface fishing)
- Tiger nuts
- Peanuts
- Lob worms, Dendrobaena worms, small red worm, and brandlings
- Bread (either punch, flake or paste)
- Casters
- Maggots
- Pinkies
- Sweetcorn
- Pellets
- Prawns and other seafoods like Mussel

The most popular loose feeds for catching Bream

- Hemp
- Water snails
- Bloodworm
- Boilie crumb/flake
- Groundbait – Base flavours of Continental/Sweet/Fishmeal/Cereal
- Sweetcorn
- Casters
- Chopped worms
- Pellets

Methods

Carp are caught using various methods including float, ledger, or feeder. There are so many methods when it comes to ledgering or fishing off the bottom with static baits. The use of PVA bags and mesh is very commonplace when fishing well stocked venues. There are also many baits for catching Carp and some Carp anglers swear using boilies. A guide to the basic tackle needed for Carp fishing is a rod with a minimum of a 2 lb test curve (or a heavy feeder rod) fitted with a fixed spool reel. The reel needs to be filled with minimum 10 lb main line and 18 – 24" 8lb hook length with a large hook. Using the 'leading' technique, find a smooth/clean patch on the lakebed, this is usually a sign of a feeding spot.

Fish safety tip! When specifically fishing for Carp, always carry and use a large unhooking mat for unhooking your fish. Often anglers who target these fish, will use cradles as well to reduce any injury to the fish. When handling larger Carp (over 30lbs) it is always best to handle them in the water, more so in hot weather. Always keep the net, mat, and cradle wet.

Top tip! When you get to your chosen swim, throw some 'free' offerings into the water where you are about to fish then get tackled up, if fishing over a couple of days, lay a bed of loose feed/groundbait to get them into the swim.

Carp – Crucian

Carassius carrasius
Cyprinidae Family

Average weight

The Crucian Carp is a medium-sized Cyprinid and usually weigh between 6 ounces and 1 lb 8 ounces (160-810 g). They can grow between 6-12" (15-30 cm) in length, and rarely exceeds in weight over 2 kg (4.4 lb) but there has been a record weight of 3 kg (6.6 lb).

Description

Although part of the same family as the common Carp, the Crucian Carp is different in that it does not have barbules. They vary in colour but mainly have a brownish colouring across the back with gold or greyish green sides. They usually have a very rounded body with a covering of small scales in an even pattern. The reddish fins of the Crucian are rounded with a convex dorsal fin. The Crucian Carp is a very hardy and extremely adaptable fish, able to survive in ponds and lakes with poor water quality with little oxygen that would prove fatal to most other species.

Habitat

It is an English still water fish, with a preference for heavily overgrown, natural ponds and small lakes. Some slow-flowing rivers and canals can hold small populations too, but quite rare. The crucian carp is a bottom feeder, it forages in the thick mud and silt on the bottom, feeding on plant life. Occasionally it will rise to the surface to take water beetles or insect larvae. A typical place for them is in the shallower regions of a pond or lake, areas with reeds, submerged weed beds and lilies.

Swim choice

Crucian Carp are found in shoals (sometimes large), often with fish of the same size or age. They are very shy biting fish and can be very easily spooked. When targeting them, fish the areas where their natural food sources would normally be near reeds or weeds in the shallow margins.

Baits and loose feeds

The most popular hook baits for catching Crucian Carp

- Dendrobaena worms, small red worm, and brandlings
- Bread (either punch, flake or paste)
- Casters
- Maggots
- Pinkies
- Sweetcorn
- Small Pellets

The most popular loose feeds for catching Crucian Carp

- Hemp
- Groundbait – Base flavours of Sweet/Fishmeal/Cereal
- Brown crumb
- Sweetcorn
- Casters
- maggots
- Chopped worms
- Pellets

Methods

As with most fish, Crucian Carp can be caught using all methods of angling including float, ledger, or feeder but the float seems best. Light tackle is the order of the day, fished on or just off the bottom near reeds or around surface plants like Lilies. Self-cocking floats, quills that require no shot to hold their position and small pole floats are ideal depending on the type of water you are fishing. Crucian carp are very smart and very wary, so shotting patterns need to be able to display very delicate bites.

Fish safety tip! They spawn once water temperatures are consistently above 18°C and usually after rainfall, so avoid fishing in these conditions to preserve breeding habits.

Top tip! When fishing with caster as bait, if hooked through the end and you get bites, and when striking you find the crucian has left you with an empty half shell, try burying the hook totally inside the caster.

Catfish - Wels

Silurus glanis
Siluridae Family

Average weight

The Wels Catfish usually grows to 47-63" (120-160 cm) long and weighs up to 110 lb (50 kg). It's rare that these fish get any bigger or heavier. Average weights are around 10–20lb (5.0kg-10.0kg) and lengths of 60cm–90cm: (24-36").

Description

The Catfish is so named for their prominent barbules that look like cats' whiskers, is the longest and heaviest freshwater fish species in the UK. Catfish look nothing like regular fish and more similar to an Eel. They have a long scale-less body, an enormous head with six 'whiskers' protruding from it and an equally enormous mouth. The fish has a large head that tapers back to the large tail with a small dorsal fin an anal fin that stretches backwards until it almost reaches the tail and paddle like pectoral fin is also very large. The mouth is filled with hundreds of tiny soft teeth on the top and bottom of its jaw that are used to grip its prey before passing it to the two sets of crushing pads at the back of the throat.

Colouration of Catfish is normally a dark green, brown, black body with creamy yellowish sides creating a mottled camouflage effect ideal for when they are hunting their prey.

Habitat

Catfish live in quiet, dark lairs in rivers and lakes until they are ready to feed. Catfish live in hollows under the bank, under hanging trees or in weed beds. They will actively hunt in the open water as well as they are both scavenger and predator and will react to a variety of baits.

Swim choice

Catfish feed mainly at night but will feed at any time and seem to favour snaggy areas. Wels Catfish can usually be found patrolling the margins or in in deep holes. They also like to be among weed beds and lilies, hiding in hollows under the bank or lurking under overhanging branches of trees.

Baits and loose feeds

The most popular hook baits for catching Catfish

- Silverfish between 4" and 12"
- Boilies
- Pellets
- Worms - Lobworms, Dendrobaena, Redworms and Brandlings
- Sea fish - Mackerel and Herring

The most popular loose feeds for catching Catfish

- Pellets
- Boilies
- Groundbait – Fishmeal based

Methods

To fish specifically for Catfish, you will need as least a 2.5 – 3.5lb test curve rod, 200m of 15lb mainline on a reel as a minimum, abrasion resistant hook links and large strong single hooks larger than a size 2. You ideally want to fish off of the bottom using a strong scented bait, the most common are hair rigged halibut pellets soaked in fish oil.

Fish over an area of small pellets and you should attract some nice fish. You can also use ledgered live bait such as Roach just below the surface using various rigs to good effect, none to dissimilar from Pike fishing.

Fish safety tip! Make sure you have an extra-large landing net, large mat, and pair of long nosed forceps for unhooking close to hand.

Top tip! Catfish can grow to a monstrous size and weight so make sure you have the tackle to cope. Strong rods, line and end tackle are a must.

Chub

Leuciscus cephalus
Cyprinidae Family

Average weight

A decent sized chub is anything between 3 lb and 5 lb (1.4-2.3 kg) and very good fight when playing it in. The British Record is 9lb 5oz and around 50cms in length.

Description

The Chub (Also known as a Chevin) is a thick set fish with a large blunt head. It has a long and cylindrical body with large greenish/brown scales that have a slight black edging across the back working down to a lighter golden flank and a light belly with a dark brown to blackish tail. The dorsal fin of the Chub is a greyish/green colour with all the other fins being orange/red. The Chub has a large mouth with thick rubbery lips and a voracious appetite and will eat almost anything. When smaller, the Chub is sometimes mistaken for Dace as both the Chub and the Dace have similar body and fin colouring. Identification between the two is by the shaping of the dorsal and anal fins. The Chub have convex shaped fins while the Dace is concave.

Habitat

The Chub is mainly a river fish, preferring moderate to fast flowing waters but are found in slow to the faster moving rivers and weirs especially where trees or bushes overhang the water. The Chub is also found in ponds and lakes and is now being stocked in commercial fisheries. The Chub is known for being gluttonous and will eat just about anything. Unlike other fish the Chub will feed throughout the year be it a hot summer afternoon or freezing winter morning.

Swim choice

The Chub prefers to lie close to cover, usually around sunken trees, overhanging branches and clumps of brambles. Look for fast glides, gentle slacks, and eddies.

Baits and loose feeds

The most popular hook baits for catching Chub

- Worms, lob worms, and redworms
- Cheese (especially the smelly cheese)
- Cheese paste
- Bread (either crust, flake or paste)
- Maggots, pinkies, and casters
- Pellets
- Hemp and tares
- Wasp grubs
- Slugs (Black Slugs are a good chub bait)
- Sweetcorn
- Luncheon meat
- Sausage meat
- Berries and elderberry
- Shrimps, cockles (fresh only)
- Boilies

The most popular loose feeds for catching Chub

- Chopped worms or loose fed
- Groundbait – Fishmeal/Meat/Cereal
- Cheese (especially the smelly cheese)
- Breadcrumbs or flake
- Maggots, pinkies, and casters
- Pellets
- Hemp and tares
- Sweetcorn
- Luncheon meat or Sausage meat
- Chopped Shrimps, cockles (fresh only)
- Boilies

Methods

Chub can be caught using various methods including float, ledger, feeder, free lining, spinning with lures and even fly fishing. A medium rod with a fixed spool reel fitted with a minimum of 3lb line should be used. Hook size of 16 to a 4 but this will depend on the size of the bait used. Essential, fishing for Chub is not too dissimilar to Barbel, just a little lighter and no hair rigs (this is mainly because the Chub pick up bait with their mouths and do not suck it in like most bottom feeders. For bigger Chub, use a bigger bait. The Chub is also caught using plugs and lures and also by fly fishing.

Fish safety tip! Once hooked, a Chub will swim straight for any rushes or underwater obstacles like submerged trees or tree roots and snag you up. Be ready to strike at any time.

Top tip! Tackle up away from your peg, Chub are very wary fish and can be spooked easily. The vibrations you make next to the water can spook the Chub and when you are stood near the water your profile against the skyline can scare them away.

Dace

Leuciscus leuciscus
Cyprinidae Family

Average weight

Dace typically weighs between 2-6 oz (0.05-0.15 kg) and can grow to an average length of between 4-6" (10-15 cm). In optimal conditions, they can reach sizes of 2.2 lb (1 kg), however, in the UK a good catch would be a specimen around 8 oz (230 g).

Description

The Dace is a fast, lively, active fish, nicknamed the Dart, because of the way it darts through the fast-flowing waters. The freshwater fish is closely related to the Chub but is a more streamlined fish and distinguished from the Chub by its anal and dorsal fins which are both concave, whereas the Chub's anal and dorsal fins are convex and red in colour. Young dace also closely resembles the Roach in appearance, both in size and shape but the Roach has red eyes and the Dace have yellow eyes. The Dace has a slender body, narrow pointed head with large yellow eyes and a small mouth, the body has greyish blue back with silvery flanks, white belly and the tail is deeply forked.

Habitat

The Dace prefers clean, well oxygenated water and can be found in shoals in mid water or the fast-flowing upper layers of water especially around weirs and weir pools. Although predominantly found in rivers and streams with a sand or gravel substrate, the Dace can also be found in lakes and still waters, probably introduced by man or through floods.

Swim choice

The Dace prefers a consistent depth of about two feet (60cm) or more and stretches for a yard or so. These make for good spots to find a shoal of Dace. With most shoals of Dace, they are made up of fish no bigger than a few ounces, but sometimes this is not always the case, which makes this form of fishing particularly exciting.

Baits and loose feeds

The most popular hook baits for catching Dace

- Casters
- Maggots, pinkies, and squats.
- Bloodworm or small red worm
- Bread - Punched or small piece of bread flake

The most popular loose feeds for catching Dace

- Casters
- Maggots, pinkies, and squats.
- Bloodworm or small red worm,
- Bread - Punched or small piece of bread flake
- Breadcrumbs or flake.

Methods

Light fishing tackle and small hooks are order of the day, the best method is stick float fishing. Because the Dace is quick to feel resistance on the line and tend to drop bait easily use the lightest stick float possible. In the summer the stick float, with shot spread evenly down the line, hook size 22 to 16 baited with single caster or maggot just below mid-water. Because of their small mouth, the main baits for catching Dace would be maggot or casters.

Fish safety tip! The Dace do not fare to well when being kept out of the water for too long, as they predominantly live in fast flowing waters. They are used to filtering a lot of oxygen, so unhooking and any photos need to be quick.

Top tip! When fishing the stick float, holding back from time to time to let the bait rise nearer to the surface is a great trick. This rise and fall of the bait will often tempt the Dace into biting.

Eel

Anguilla anguilla
Anguillidae Family

Average weight

The average length of an adult eel in the UK is between 20-30" (60-80cm) with an average weight of between 2.2-4.4 lbs (1-2 kg). The females grow larger than the males and in optimal conditions can reach impressive lengths of up to 4 feet (1.2m) and weigh up to 20 lbs (9kg).

Description

The Eel has an elongated body similar to that of a snake and a longish head with rounded eyes. The eyes are small in young Eels and large in older and silver Eels. The Eel has a protruding lower jaw longer than the upper jaw. The teeth are small and set in bands in both jaws and in a patch on vomer. Small and vertical gill openings restricted to the sides. The dorsal fin originates far behind the pectoral fins and the dorsal and anal fins confluent with caudal fin. The anal fin set slightly behind anus, well back from origin of dorsal fin. The pectoral fins of the Eel are small and rounded. Lateral line conspicuous. It has minute elliptical scales embedded in the skin.

Habitat

Eels are found in almost all waters but angling for them in still waters that are known to hold them is your best option. The best time to catch Eels is early dawn or at dusk and through the night but they can be caught throughout the day.

Swim choice

Look for rich waters, with weed beds and plenty of invertebrate life. Eels love snags, like fallen trees, weed beds and undercuts are ideal locations to place baits. Marginal areas should not be overlooked as they may patrol these areas looking for dead or dying fish and food items that may be washed up or windblown. Areas where fry or prey fish congregate or where fish spawn are excellent hotspots.

Baits and loose feeds

The most popular hook baits for catching Eel

- Dead bait section
- Worms - lob worms
- Maggots and casters

The most popular loose feeds for catching Eel

- Maggots
- Dead bait sections
- Groundbait – Coarse/Cereal/Fishmeal

Methods

Various methods including float, ledger or feeder are used to catch Eels and float fishing with a waggler over a bed of groundbait, slightly over depth close to reeds is a good tactic. The feeder is also considered a good method as is ledgering, also a preferred method for Eel fishing.

Match, float, or feeder rods can be used with a reel filled with 4 lb main line. 3 lb hook length and size 16 or 14 hook would be a good starting point

Fish safety tip! When you hook an Eel, especially a small Eel (Also known as a bootlace), it will almost certainly curl up and get tangled in your line. It will also make a mess of your line with the slime from its body. To unhook an eel there are unhooking tubes, a tube of approximately 1.5 or 2-inch diameter and a foot long with a slit along the side. The idea is to hold your line taut and slide the tube onto it via the slit and then slide the tube down over the eel until its head appears and unhook it.

Top tip! They respond very well to heavy groundbaiting and sometimes, when groundbaiting for other fish, you will end up catching an Eel.

Grayling

Thymallus thymallus
Salmonidae Family

Average weight

The average Grayling in the UK is between 8-11" (20-30 cm) in length and weighs around 6oz-1 lb (0.15-0.5 kg). A good catch would be in the region of 2 lbs (0.9 kg), but records have shown fish over 4lbs (1.6kg)

Description

Grayling, also known as, 'the Lady of the Stream', are members of the Salmon family and are considered by some anglers as coarse fish and by others as game fish. With their huge dorsal fin Grayling are unmistakable from other fish. The Grayling is a streamlined fish with a small, pointed head, silvery blue body with thin silver / violet stripes and irregular dark spots on the flanks. The Grayling is a shoaling fish very sensitive to pollution and are generally found in clean, fast flowing, well oxygenated freshwater streams and small rivers with gravel or chalk beds. Males tend to have much bigger rounder dorsal fins.

Habitat

Whilst grayling can be found throughout the UK, they are most abundant in clean, oxygenated waters, usually fast flowing, gravel bottomed rivers and streams. The diet of this species varies based on where it lives and what food is available. They are omnivorous, which means that they eat both plant and animal matter. In addition to algae and underwater vegetation, it also feeds on insects, plankton, insect larvae, small fish, shrimp, crabs, and more.

Swim choice

The Grayling is often found in the deeper reaches of the rivers that they inhabit. When they begin feeding, they glide upwards and ambush their prey from below. They also tend to be in shoals, so catching one means that if you stick around, you're likely to land another at least, providing you do not spook them off.

Baits and loose feeds

The most popular hook baits for catching Grayling

- Maggots
- Worms
- Artificial flies.
- Bread

The most popular loose feeds for catching Grayling

- Maggots
- Worms
- Breadcrumb

Methods

Grayling can be caught all year, but the best fishing is noted to be best on a clear, cold winters day, although any time from autumn through winter can be very productive. Grayling feed mainly on the bottom but will feed from the surface when mayfly and nymphs are about. Fly fishing is a great way to catch Grayling but fishing the stick float and trotting it down stream is also a very effective method. Using a light to medium rod with a 4lb mainline and 3lb hook length, trot a small worm or 2 or 3 maggots on a size 16 hook down the stream. Fishing with a light feeder with 4lb or 5lb main line, small block end feeder loaded with maggots can also be effective. 3lb hook length of 12 to 24" with 2 or 3 maggots on a size 16 hook or a worm on a size 14 hook.

Fish safety tip! The Grayling, similar to the Dace, do not fare to well when being kept out of the water for too long, as they predominantly live in fast flowing waters. Hold the fish, in the net, facing upstream in a reasonable flow until it is capable of swimming on balance and under its own power. Never move any fish back and forth in the water - it can cause serious damage.

Top tip! The bigger Graylings seem to be caught on worms and a good fish is around a pound and 2 lb or over considered a specimen. Use a small piece of float rubber pushed onto the hook, this will help keep the worm from coming off if you are using barbless or micro barbed hooks.

Gudgeon

Gobio gobio
Cyprinidae Family

Average weight

An average Gudgeon weighs between 1-2 oz (30-60 g) and is between 3-4" (7-12 cm) in length. Anything above 2oz (60 g) would be considered an impressive specimen.

Description

The Gudgeon is sometimes mistaken for small baby barbel but can very easily be identified. The Gudgeon has two barbels (whisker like protrusions) one on either side of its mouth as opposed to the barbel which has two either side and the stone loach which has six. Gudgeon are bottom feeders and these barbels are used to search for food on the riverbed (lake, canal, or water it lives in). It has a rounded, elongated body with a slightly flattened belly and rather large scale less head with an under slung mouth with thick lips. Both dorsal and anal fins are short and heavily spotted.
Coloration of the Gudgeon is silvery blue or green, brown on the back with a row of large, dark spots on the yellowish flanks.

Habitat

Predominantly found in rivers or fast-moving streams, the Gudgeon can be found in most waters. The Gudgeon is noted as preferring the faster running waters with a gravel bottom where they search for food. They are a shoal fish often found in large shoals. Catch one and you are likely to catch many more.

Swim choice

Slower areas just off the main flow are great spots to catch Gudgeon, they also like back eddies where the current swirls back on itself. Whilst fishing such an area may not look ideal, it is actually an effective way to catch Gudgeon.

Baits and loose feeds

The most popular hook baits for catching Gudgeon

- Maggot, pinkie, or caster
- Red worm, brandling, or bloodworm
- Bread - bread punch

The most popular loose feeds for catching Gudgeon

- Maggot, pinkie, or caster
- Red worm, brandling, or bloodworm
- Bread – breadcrumb or flake
- Groundbait – Coarse/Cereal/Fishmeal/Match

Methods

Fished for on the bottom with light tackle using the humble maggot for bait they fight reasonably well for their size. Any method can be adopted for catching Gudgeon but fishing with light tackle is more productive and more fun. With Gudgeon being a bottom feeding fish the first choice in catching them is probably ledgering. Try float fishing with maggot or any of the baits listed, on or just off the bottom.

Fish safety tip! When fishing for Gudgeon, be aware that the same tactics can catch other species such as Perch or Roach. So be prepared to adjust how you play the fish, loose feeding will bring most species in for a feed.

Top tip! Once you start catching, keep the fish interested by loose feeding. Groundbait can also be used but make sure this is mixed so that is sinks to the bottom before breaking up or you may disperse the shoal.

Minnow

Phoxinus phoxinus
Cyprinidae Family

Average weight

The average size of the common Minnow is 4-10 cm. The average weight is 8-16 g. Average Lifespan is around 2-5 years.

Description

It is a small fish with a flat sided body. It has a semi pointed head with large eyes and a small mouth that is turned upwards.
The Minnow is olive-brown above, with dark bars along its back and a dark stripe down its side. Females have silver bellies, but the males' bellies turn pinkish red in the summer. They are the third smallest native fish after the 9 spine and 3 spine Stickleback, but the Minnow lacks the dorsal spines of sticklebacks.

Habitat

Minnow can be found in most streams, and the slower moving rivers and rarely in open waters. It is a shoal fish and often found in quite large shoals, living, and feeding in the upper layers of the water on insects, molluscs, crustaceans, plant debris and fish eggs.

Swim choice

On smaller rivers and streams, the Minnow can be found in shoals, mainly in the well covered parts of the water.

Baits and loose feeds

The most popular hook baits for catching Minnow

- Maggot
- Pinkies
- Caster
- Small red worm
- Brandling
- Pieces of worm
- Small pieces of bread, and bread punch

The most popular loose feeds for catching Minnow

- Hemp
- Groundbait – Base flavours of Fishmeal/Sweet/Cereal
- Castors and Maggots
- Chopped worm
- Breadcrumb

Methods

Minnow can be caught on light float tackle. Using a float rod or whip, place most of the shot under the float so that the bait falls through the water slowly. Using maggot as bait, put 1 or 2 on a size 16 to 20 hook. With a shoal of Minnow nearby, you will find that bites come fast and furious. A few loose fed maggots will keep them interested.

Fish safety tips! Due to these fish having very small mouths, try not to allow the bites to over develop as unhooking them can be fatal, as they swallow the hook and bait too deeply. Ensure you have a small hook disgorger to hand. When handling the fish be aware that the scales are loose and very easily dislodged.

Top tip! The Minnow is not usually targeted by the general angler but because they swim in large shoals and are easy to catch the match angler can soon whip up a big weight. Like the Gudgeon, and the Bleak, they have saved the day for many a match angler from blanking.

Perch

Perca fluviatilis
Percidae Family

Average weight

The average Perch in the UK grows between 4-10" (12-25 cm) in length and weigh between 4-12 oz (250-750 g). A perch weighing 1lb (0.45 kg) would be considered a very decent catch, with specimens between 2-3 lbs (0.9-1.4 kg) becoming more common.

Description

The perch has a flat sided greenish body graduating down to a white belly. It has bright red/orange pelvic fins, two dorsal fins and five or more broad black vertical stripes down the sides of its body. It has a row of sharp pointed spines along the dorsal fin so be careful when handling it. The body of the perch is rough to the touch as the small scales are imbedded deep in the skin. The perch will probably be the first fish an angler catches because they are a very aggressive predator that will bite at almost anything, so often when float fishing for smaller silver fish with bait such as red maggot, you will very likely catch a small Perch of a few ounces.

Habitat

The Perch lives in still, slow, and fast running waters, lakes, ponds, rivers and canals and they can be found where there is underwater obstacles or structures such as tree roots, weed beds and overhanging trees as they are all good places to hide and ambush anything edible.

Swim choice

They like to lay in wait in and around sub-surface features such as tree roots, overhanging branches, reed beds, aquatic weed beds, undercut banks and man-made structures such as bridge stanchions. The Perch is gregarious, and as temperatures drop in the autumn and winter months, fish of different sizes shoal and move into deeper water, with colder temperatures bring about little activity and they feed very little. As a result, fish close to any features in the shallower areas during the warmer months with deeper areas more likely to hold the fish in the autumn and winter.

Baits and loose feeds

The most popular hook baits for catching Perch

- Lob worms, Dendrobaena worms, red worm, and brandlings
- Casters
- Maggots
- Live bait/dead bait – such as Minnows
- Artificial baits
- Plugs, lures, and spinners.
- Artificial flies

The most popular loose feeds for catching Perch

- Chopped worm
- Maggots
- Casters
- Groundbait - Fishmeal

Methods

Perch can be caught using various fishing methods including float, ledger, feeder, free lining, spinning with lures, drop shot fishing and even fly fishing. For general fishing, a medium 10ft or 12 ft rod with a fixed spool reel fitted with 3 or 4lb line, hook size of 16 or larger depending on the bait used is ok. On still waters, lakes, and ponds, try float fishing using a waggler with a big lobworm on a size 10 hook. Plumb the depth and fish over depth by 6". Use chopped worm mixed in with your groundbait and throw a couple of balls in at the start.

Fish safety tips! The Perch as mentioned above, has a row of sharp pointed spines along the dorsal fin so be careful when handling it. Also, the gill covers have sharp points on too, so always handle from underneath the area near the gills to avoid this.

Top tip! If you are fishing with lobworms, after hooking the lobworm, pinch off the end of the tail of the worm and put this on the hook; this makes the worm wriggle more and releases a scent into the water which will hopefully attract the perch. If you don't get a bite after a few minutes, try twitching your bait (reel in a couple of turns) this sometimes induces the Perch to bite. If you know there is an underwater feature in your swim, cast near to this.

Pike

Esox lucius
Esocidae family

Average weight

Average Pike in the UK usually weigh between 5-11lbs and have an average length of 22-35" (55-85 cm). However, they live for many years and continue to grow throughout their lives, specimens of 35 lbs plus are caught each year.

Description

The Pike is unmistakable with its distinguished striped or spotted pattern body, large broad head, flattened snout and huge mouth full of sharp, backward facing teeth. Its long torpedo shaped camouflaged body which is built for speed, and its dorsal and anal fins are set far back, much further than most other fish. Pike will eat most other species of fish and almost anything that moves in or on the water. Larger pike will even eat smaller pike.

Habitat

The Pike inhabits nearly all types of waters, preferring those waters that are still or slow moving. The main requirement for big pike is a healthy supply of shoal fish for the pike to feed on, so well stocked venues with a good body of water will hold some larger specimens. In warmer water temperatures, the prey fish will be spread out.

Swim choice

Look for drop-offs which are noted holding points for the predators such as pike as they can hold in the deeper water, waiting for prey fish to move in or out of the shallows before they strike. Also, check any kind of structure as these tend to hold pike. Usually in the shallower areas, meaning the pike could be anywhere. In the colder temperatures, mainly in autumn and winter, the Roach and Bream that pike eat will look for a more constant temperature in deeper water and so will shoal together in these places... and the pike will not be far away.

Baits and loose feeds

The most popular hook baits for catching Pike

- Live bait - silver fish
- Dead bait - Mackerel, Roach, Trout, Herring, Smelt and Sardine
- Artificial Lure
- Plugs
- Artificial Soft bait
- Crankbait

Methods

A variety of methods can be used when fishing for Pike including spinning with lures, live baiting, and dead baiting. A favourite method with most pike anglers is ledgering with a dead bait. Fishing for Pike requires fishing tackle similar to Carp fishing. A powerful rod and strong line, with the addition of a wire trace. A good rod for Pike fishing should have a test curve of 2.5lb or more. Wire traces are essential when fishing for Pike because they have very sharp teeth and would almost certainly bite through ordinary line. Main line needs to be around 15lb with a wire trace of 30lb and 12" to 18" in length. Hooks are usually treble or double varieties.

Fish safety tips! The pike have sharp teeth and clamp down on your hand when unhooking, always use a soft and careful grip on the gills so you can unhook the fish. The internals of the gills are soft, so please make sure your hands are wet and clean.

Top tip! If the pike is deep hooked or you have difficulty in removing a treble hook it might be better for the pike if you use a pair of side cutters to cut the hook up and remove it in two or more pieces.

Roach

Rutilus Rutilus
Cyprinidae Family

Average weight

Small fish up to 1lb are commonplace and a fish of over 2lb is seen as a specimen. 3lb fish are rare from rivers, but a number of southern still waters regularly throw up quality fish close to the 4lb barrier.

Description

A moderately deep bodied fish with silvery white sides and back of dark brown or grey with a bluish or greenish tint, red eyes, large silvery scales, and orange/red lower fins, hence the nickname, Redfin. The Roach is found in shoals just about everywhere, in lakes, ponds, rivers and canals. Growing to over 4lb a fish of 2lb is considered excellent and 3lb considered a specimen. The Roach is commonly mistaken for Rudd, but you can tell the difference between them as the Rudd has an upturned mouth as opposed to the Roach which facing forwards and can extend downwards if they are heavy bottom feeders. The colour of the Rudd is also more golden and a lot brighter than Roach.

Habitat

The Roach is an extremely versatile species of fish and is one of the most widely distributed fish in the UK. As such it can be caught in pretty much any waterway, from small ponds to the largest lakes and rivers that the UK has to offer. The larger Roach is particularly elusive and prefer habitats with aquatic vegetation, more so when the spawning begins.

Swim choice

You can catch Roach from all depths of the water column, but the biggest specimens are caught at the bottom. As with many silver fish, they are prime targets for predation, so fish will be in shoals near and around any form of shelter. Overhanging trees or bushes, and where the river deepens, and the flow slows are fantastic spots for large Roach. With slower waters, look just off the main current, along reed beds are also good Roach spots.

Baits and loose feeds

The most popular hook baits for catching Roach

- Casters
- Maggot
- Hemp and Tares
- Bread flake
- Worms - small brandling or pieces of worm
- Sweetcorn
- Cocktail with a worm or red maggot

The most popular loose feeds for catching Roach

- Groundbait – Continental/Fishmeal/Cereal/Match
- Casters
- Maggot
- Hemp and Tares
- Bread flake
- Chopped worms
- Sweetcorn

Methods

All methods including float, leger or feeder are options for Roach fishing, but the float seems most popular. Whatever the method is chosen, light tackle with small hooks is the order of the day. Roach can be caught at any time of day and in the summer, they seem to feed best early in the morning or late in the afternoon. In the winter and during the colder months Roach will move into the deeper parts of the lakes, and a good time to try is from late afternoon to dusk.

A basic float set up for Stillwater Roach is 3 to 3.5lb mainline, 3AAA waggler with a size 18 - 16 hook on 1.5lb hook length.

Fish safety tips! Try not to allow the bites to over develop as unhooking them can be difficult, as they swallow the hook and bait too deeply. Ensure you have a small hook disgorger to hand.

Top tip! Bites from Roach can be very fast, so you have to be ready to strike.

Rudd

Scardinius erythrophthalmus
Cyprinidae Family

Average weight

The average Rudd in the UK usually weighs between 2-8 oz (50-200g). Sizes of 3- 4lb can be found in well stocked lakes, with records reaching over 4lb.

Description

The body of the Rudd is flattened at the sides, the back is blue-green and the belly a silvery white; the dorsal fin and pectoral fins are reddish-grey, and all other fins are a deep red. Rudd can be identified by the dorsal fin which is set further back and starts behind an imaginary vertical line projected upwards from the pelvic fins. The eyes have yellow to orange irises compared to a Roach which is red. The mouth of the Rudd curves upwards as opposed to Roach which protrude downwards.

Habitat

Rudd tend to be a shoaling fish usually living in the lower reaches of rivers, backwaters, and ponds with plenty of aquatic vegetation and profusely overgrown. Natural foods of Rudd include snails, worms, bloodworm, insects, larvae of aquatic insects, algae, shrimps, and small crustaceans. Feeding in the upper layers of the water Rudd are often seen taking flies from the surface and insects which have fallen into the water.

Swim choice

Evenings tend to be the best time to catch Rudd, as they can usually be seen dimpling at the surface. Similar to the Roach, overhanging trees or bushes, and where the water deepens are good spots for large Rudd. With slower waters, look just off the main current, along reed beds are also good Rudd spots.

Baits and loose feeds

The most popular hook baits for catching Rudd

- Casters
- Maggot
- Hemp and Tares
- Bread flake
- Worms - small brandling or pieces of worm
- Sweetcorn
- Cocktail with a worm or red maggot

The most popular loose feeds for catching Rudd

- Groundbait – Continental/Fishmeal/Cereal/Match
- Casters
- Maggot
- Hemp and Tares
- Bread flake
- Chopped worms
- Sweetcorn

Methods

Fishing for Rudd is similar to fishing for Roach and the baits used for catching Rudd are the same as used for Roach. Float fishing with a small waggler float rigged with light tackle and small fine wire hooks is considered the best method for fishing for Rudd.

Fish safety tips! As with the Roach, try not to allow the bites to over develop as unhooking them can be difficult, as they swallow the hook and bait too deeply. Ensure you have a small hook disgorger to hand.

Top tip! When fishing with caster, the Rudd, just like the Roach can bite at your caster and leave you with an empty shell. burying the hook totally inside the caster is worth a try and might be the answer to hooking the fish.

Tench

Tinca tinca
Cyprinidae Family

Average weight

In the UK, the average Tench typically grow between 16-28" (40-70cm) in length and weigh between 2-5 lb (1-2 kg). A fish of over 3lb is thought to be a good catch. The male Tench over 5lb is considered to be a specimen and are prized as good fighters, but records show 11lb+ in well stocked lakes and a current record of around 15lb.

Description

The Tench is very easily identified by their thick set, well rounded, dark olive-green coloured body, sometimes looking almost black. There is also golden, yellow, and orange Tench, but these are mainly found in ornamental ponds. The scales are very tiny which give the appearance of the fish actually being scale-less. The fins are rounded, and the caudal fin is large almost paddle like. The Tench is sometimes called the 'doctor fish' because other fish would deliberately rub against them and be cured of their ailments with the slime from the Tench, which was thought to have healing properties.

Habitat

The Tench is known to feed in the margins, among reeds, lily beds and other features. Found in slow running rivers and canals but more often found in still waters, lakes, ponds.

Swim choice

The Tench prefers still waters, with clay or muddy bottoms with plenty of underwater vegetation. If you are fishing on a venue where Carp are being caught, it is likely that you'll find Tench in the same place. You can sometimes locate them by the bubbles which they create through their gills as they search the mud for food. The bubbles will form in wavy lines.

Baits and loose feeds

The most popular hook baits for catching Tench

- Sweetcorn
- Worm
- Bread, - punch, flake or paste
- Maggots, caster, and pinkies
- Mini boilies
- Pellets
- Prawns
- Cockles and mussels (not pickled in vinegar).

The most popular loose feeds for catching Tench

- Groundbait – Continental/Fishmeal/Match
- Hemp
- Pellets
- Boilie crumbs or flake
- Breadcrumb

Methods

Tench love patrolling the margins and around lily beds and reeds so fishing with a waggler, set slightly over depth, close to reeds is a good proven tactic. Tench bites are usually a couple of knocks or small lifts on the float then it slides away slowly under the water. Some anglers prefer using a maggot or method feeder and sit waiting for that slow pull round of the rod tip to say there is a fish on. A new technique is the worm kebab, this is a hair rigged bait stop on a size 10-12 hook, this approach can be very effective when feeder
fishing chopped worm.

Fish safety tips! They should be handled with care to ensure that their fins, skin, and scales are undamaged. A quality wet unhooking mat will ensure that they are protected. Use a good landing net to bring the fish in.

Top tip! The best time to catch Tench is either early dawn or at dusk and through the night. they feed almost exclusively on the bottom, and you can spot Tench feeding by the stream of tiny bubbles that can be seen bubbling on the surface of the water, as well as the muddy area of water discoloured by the Tench rooting around for food.

Zander

Sander (Stizostedion) lucioperca
Percidae family

Average weight

The average Zander in the UK weighs around 8 lb (3.6 kg) and is between 65-90 cm (25-35") in length. A small zander found in a shoal will weigh 1-3 lb (0.4-1.2 kg). A zander above 10 lbs (4.5 kg) would be considered a prime specimen.

Description

It has a tough, muscular body which is long and somewhat resembles that of the pike. Its back is green, brown in colour, the flanks are similar to Perch with dark vertical stripes and its underbelly is cream-white. The Zander has powerful jaws and long sharp teeth, the front two are particularly long. The eyes are large and in murky waters, often turn opaque to allow the Zander to spot its prey. It possesses the same distinctive double dorsal fin as the Perch. The front part is spikey, with 14 tough, sharp spines whilst the rear area of the dorsal fin is long, soft, and convex in shape. It also has a flat spine on the rear of the gill cover. The tail fin is dark whilst the pectoral, pelvic and anal fins are all an off-white colour.

Habitat

The Zander thrives in large, well oxygenated waters such as reservoirs, gravel pits and large rivers. They are most abundant in Southeast area of the UK, although in recent years have been introduced into other regions and countries across Europe. The Zander is not as widely distributed as either pike or perch, but large populations do exist in some rivers and canals.

Swim choice

The Zander are exceptional predators, preferring murky, heavily coloured waters in which to find their prey. They like to prowl around bridges and other structures, as the reduced light levels in the water below allow them to hunt more effectively. Presenting your bait slightly further upstream of a bridge is a great tactic to employ when out fishing for zander. Also fishing off a boat in large lakes and reservoirs, using drop shot techniques or artificial lures is a good way to find them.

Baits and loose feeds

The most popular hook baits for catching Zander

- Shrimps and mussels
- Dead baits - Roach, sections of Eel or Lamprey
- Artificial Lure
- Spoon lures
- Jig baits
- Crank baits

Methods

Ideal tackle you would use for catching pike, would be more than idle when after zander. A rod with a test curve between 1.75-2.75 lb will work, with a spinning reel loaded with 10-15 lb monofilament line if ledgering if float fishing use 40-50 lb braided line.

Tackle which is on the lighter end of this scale will work, but if you are able to, opt for heavier tackle. Big zander will require a heavy bait and if you're using light tackle that will make casting a challenge. A hook size between 6-8 is perfect for Zander. Smaller hooks than size 8 will only really be between 1-4 lb. Zander do have fairly small mouths in comparison to a Pike, but they're not small.

Lure fishing for Zander is a very effective technique, particularly jig fishing and can provide a great day by the water. Lure fishing from the bank will work, but the best way to catch Zander when lure fishing is to fish from a boat for them.

Jig fishing is a very tactile method of fishing which requires a fair bit of skill. The Zander responds well to simple, short raises of the lure. Lift the rod just off the bottom, or not even moving the rod at all and letting the flowing water move it for you. The Zander tends to take the bait as it falls and an echo sounder is a great tool as it lets you see where the shoals are, as well as the jig itself.

Fish safety tips! As with the Pike, be careful of the teeth. You can't really grip this is the same way as a pike, it would be more like a Perch, so adequate care and being prepared is key.

Top tip! Although you will be targeting Zander remember that Pike can also go for the same bait. you will therefore need good strong tackle in the event that you accidentally hook a Pike.

Caution: Zander have been illegally introduced into many of the UK's waterways. By law, Zander cannot be returned to the British canal network.

Knot Knowledge

A guide to tying fishing knots

How to connect two lines together – Yucatan knot

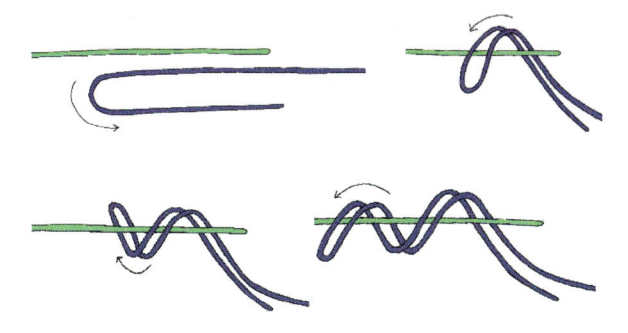

Overlap the two lines to be joined, creating a long loop with one of them. Using the loop, Wrap it around other line.

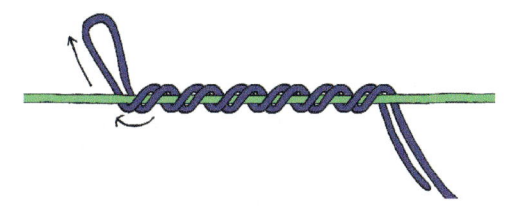

Wrap the loop around the other line 6 times

Feed the end of the other line through the loop at the end of the wrapped line. Moisten and slowly pull in opposite directions, pull tight then trim the ends to around 3mm.

How to connect two lines together – Albright knot

Make a loop in the main line (or heaviest line) and feed through around 10" of the other line through the loop.

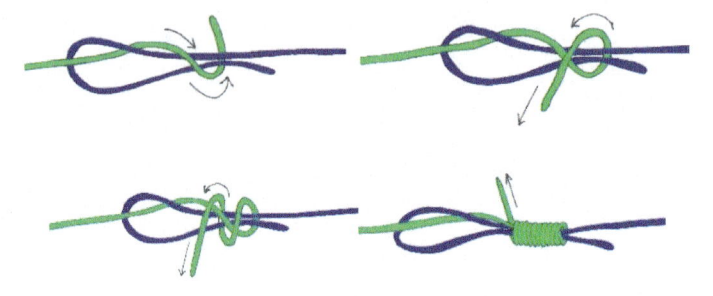

Hold the loop and the other line together. with the line that was fed through, wrap the line round the loop and back on to itself 10 times.

Feed the end of the wrapped line back through the loop and wrap both one half of the loop and the other line 5 more times.

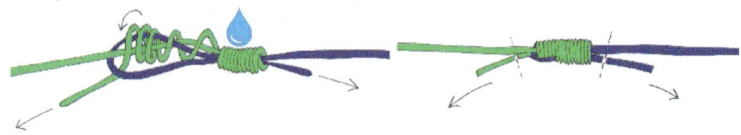

Moisten and slowly pull the lines in opposite directions, starting with the wrapped line first to cinch it together, then moisten. Now pull both lines tight and trim the tag ends to around 3mm.

How to connect two lines together – Blood knot

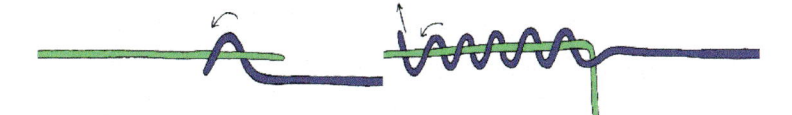

Overlap the end of the lines to be joined together. Wrap one around the other 5 times.

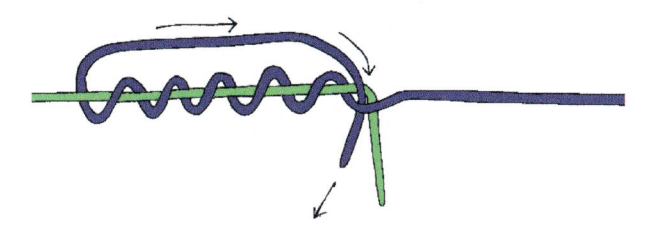

Bring the tag end back between the 2 lines (the first turn).

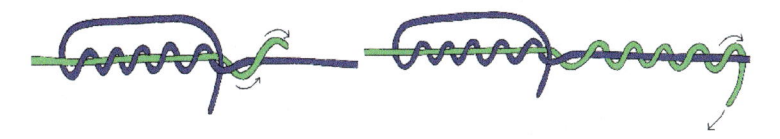

Repeat the process with the other end, wrapping in the opposite direction 5 times.

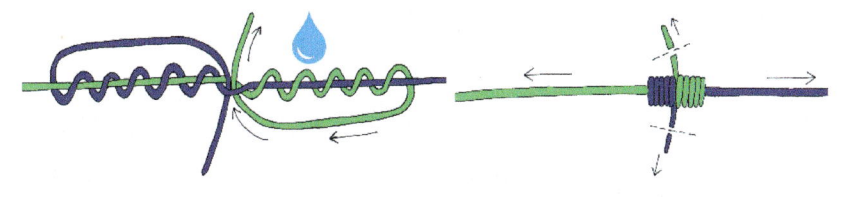

Slowly pull the lines in opposite directions, moisten, and pull tight.

Trim the tag ends by around 3mm.

How to connect two lines together – Loop to loop

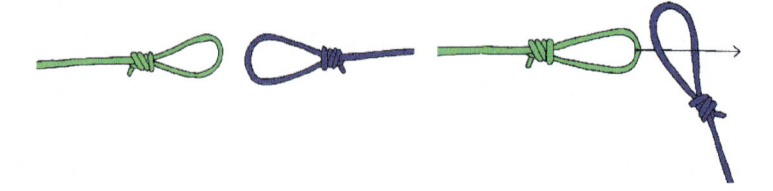

Slip the loop made of the weaker breaking (Normally a premade hook length) strain line over the other, as shown above.

Feed the end of the weaker line through the loop of the stronger line (if this is a hook length, then pass the hook through).

Pull the lines in opposite directions to lock the loops together.

Top tip! Ensure that the loops join correctly and form together. Make sure that one of the loops doesn't fold back on itself, as it can form something called a 'girth hitch' and can be a weaker link.

How to tie a loop – Overhand loop knot

Fold the line in two to start forming a long loop.

Loop it back onto itself and fold over, feeding the looped end through the newly formed loop. Tease the looped end through and adjust the loop to desired size then moisten.

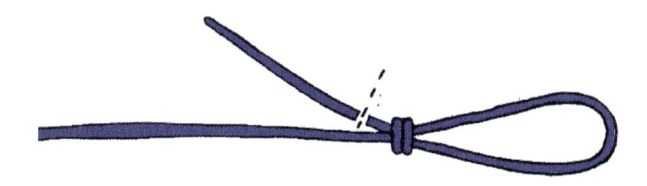

Tighten down the knot and trim the tag end to around 3mm.

Top tip! This loop knot is also used for the loops in the hair rig method for attaching a large bait to a hook.

How to tie a loop – Double overhand loop knot

Fold the line in two to start forming a long loop.

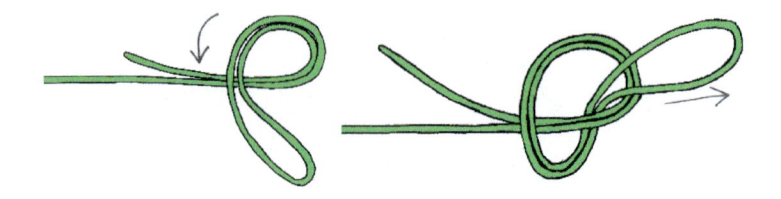

Loop it back onto itself and fold over, feeding the looped end through the newly formed loop.

Repeat the step of feeding the looped end through the newly formed loop. Tease the looped end through and adjust the loop to desired size then moisten.

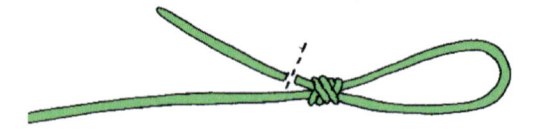

Tighten down the knot and trim the tag end to around 3mm.

How to tie a loop – Figure of 8 loop knot

Fold the line in two to start forming a long loop.

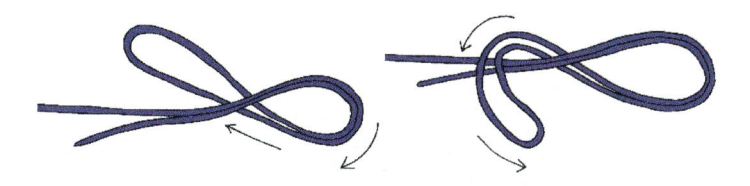

Take the looped end and then loop it back under itself (behind, not over), then fold it over the two lines.

Now feed the looped end thought the first loop created, from underneath and gently pull through. Moisten and tease the knot down so it starts to tighten.

Full tighten the loop knot (use a loop pulling tool) and trim off the excess to around 3mm.

How to tie hooks and swivels – Tucked half-blood knot

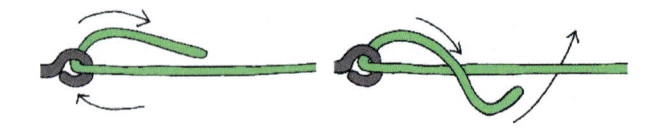

Feed line through the eye of the hook or swivel, then pull through back up the line.

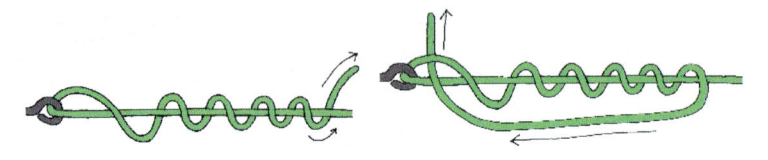

Wrap it around the line, leading away from the eye six times. Feed it back through the small loop created between the eye and the first wrap.

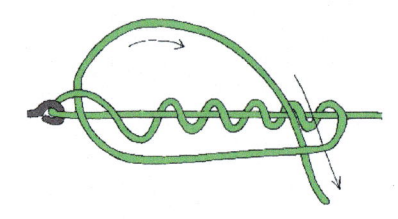

Take the line that you fed through and feed it back through between the line fed back and the wrapped line.

Now pull on both ends and tighten down the know, moisten, and tease the knot down so it starts to pull itself tight. Full tighten the knot down and trim off the tag end to around 3mm.

How to tie hooks and swivels – Grinner (Uni) knot

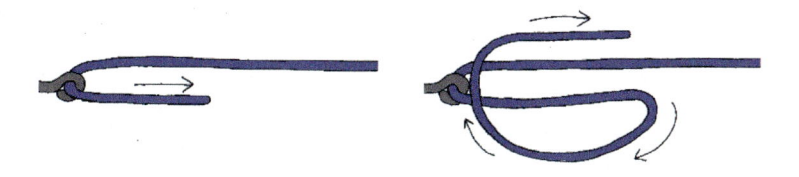

Pass the line through the eye of the hook or swivel. Using the line that was fed through the eye, fold it back towards the eye, forming a small loop as shown.

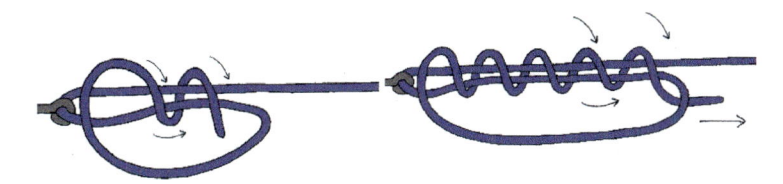

Now wrap around both the main line before being fed through the eye, and the first section line that was fed through the eye five times. Ensure that the line exits the loop and not outside of it.

Moisten the knot and gently tighten it by pulling alternately on the tag end and the main line.

Tighten down fully and trim tag end to around 3mm.

How to tie hooks and swivels – Palomar knot

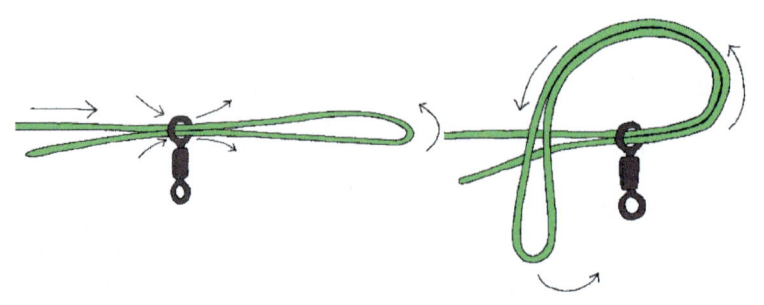

Form a long loop with the line, feed the loop through the eye of the hook or swivel and wrap it back round to the line, to form a loop.

Using the overhand knot method, feed the looped end into the loop, ensure the loop is a good size and isn't tight. Feed the hook or swivel through the looped end, moisten the knot, and gently tighten down.

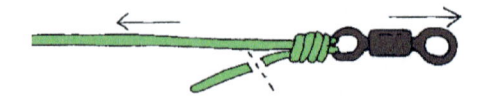

Now pull down tight. Trim the tag end to around 3mm.

Top Tip: If using a small hook, feed the line through once, then feed it back through keeping a loop formed.

How to tie hooks and swivels – Knotless knot (Hair rig)

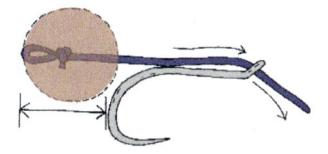

Tie a loop at the end of a section of hook link material to hold the bait on (small overhand loop knot is best). With the opposite end of the line, feed it at the back of the hook and through the eye,

adjust the length of the hair rig as required.

Now double back and make 5-8 wraps down the shank of the hook trapping the fed line from before.

After the last wrap, whilst hold the last turn, feed it back through the hook eye. Moisten and pull tight.

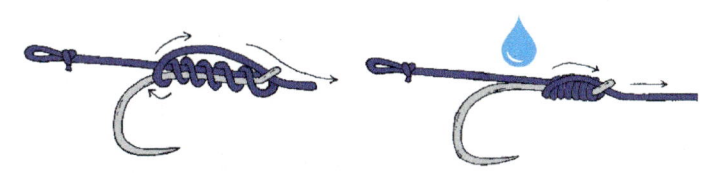

Top tip: Use some shrink wrap to cover the eye of the hook and the wrapped line of the knot, an even smaller piece can help position the hook bait (*see Bait basics section*).

How to tie other knots - Sliding stop knot

Lay a 6" length of chosen line alongside your mainline.

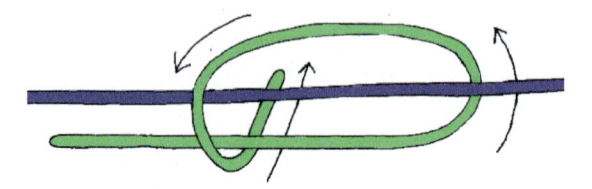

Form a loop with the chosen line and wrap one end around the loop and wrap it over the mainline.

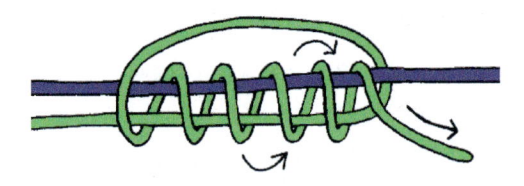

Wrap it around the same part of the loop as before and the mainline, repeat this so that the line is wrapped 5 times.

Moisten the knot, slide it into position and pull both ends tight. Trim the tag ends to round 3mm. Now the knot can be pushed into position as needed.

How to tie other knots – Arbor knot

This knot is perfect for connecting line to a reel.

Take the end of the line and tie a basic overhand knot. Moisten and tighten down. Trim the tag end to around 2mm.

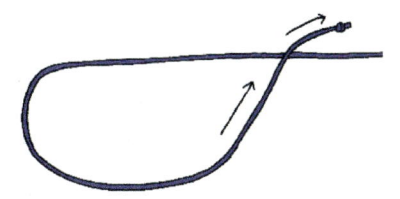

Now create a large loop of around 3" by folding the line together.

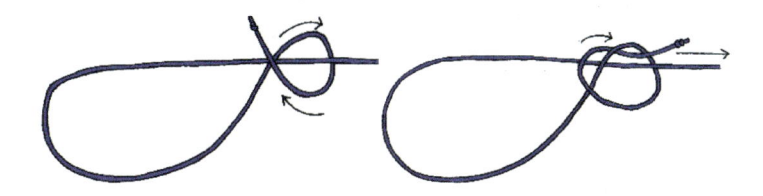

With the end of the line (with the overhand knot) tie another overhand knot but trapping the other part of the line within it.

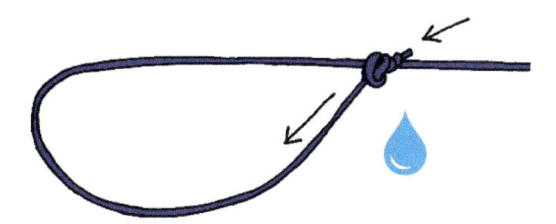

Moisten the knot and tighten it down.

Float Fishing

A guide to popular rigs used to catch fish

How to attach a float

With the waggler float or a float that has a small connecting stem with a hole through it, the mainline is thread through it. You can also use float adapters, these make it easier to changeover floats during the session without stripping down the rig.

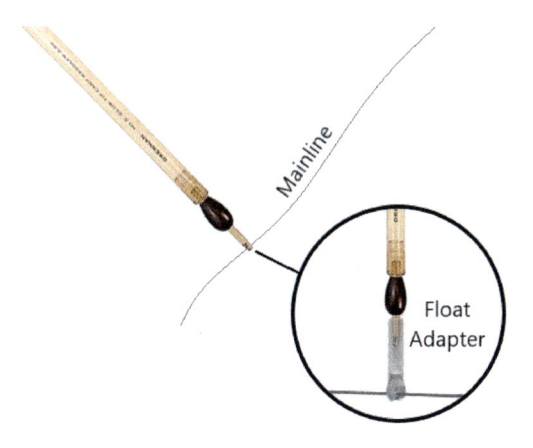

Once the float has been threaded onto the mainline, you will need to either tie a figure of 8 loop knot to attach the hooklength or use a quick connector.

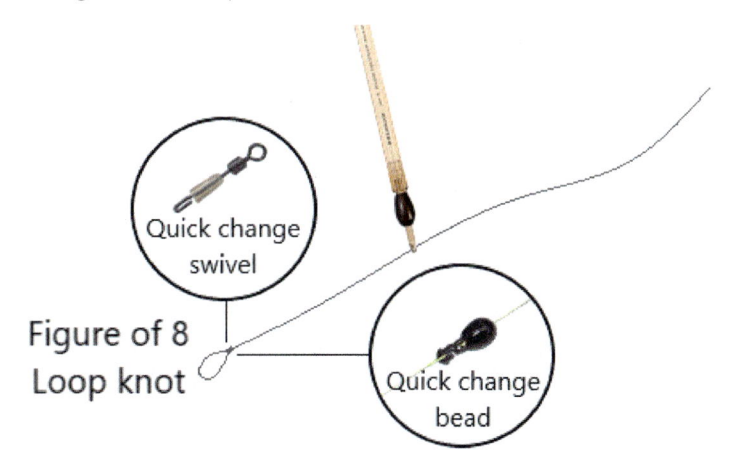

Load rating

Use shot that is below the load rating to set the float correctly

The rest of the weight is used further down the line

Pinch

Hooklength is weaker than the mainline

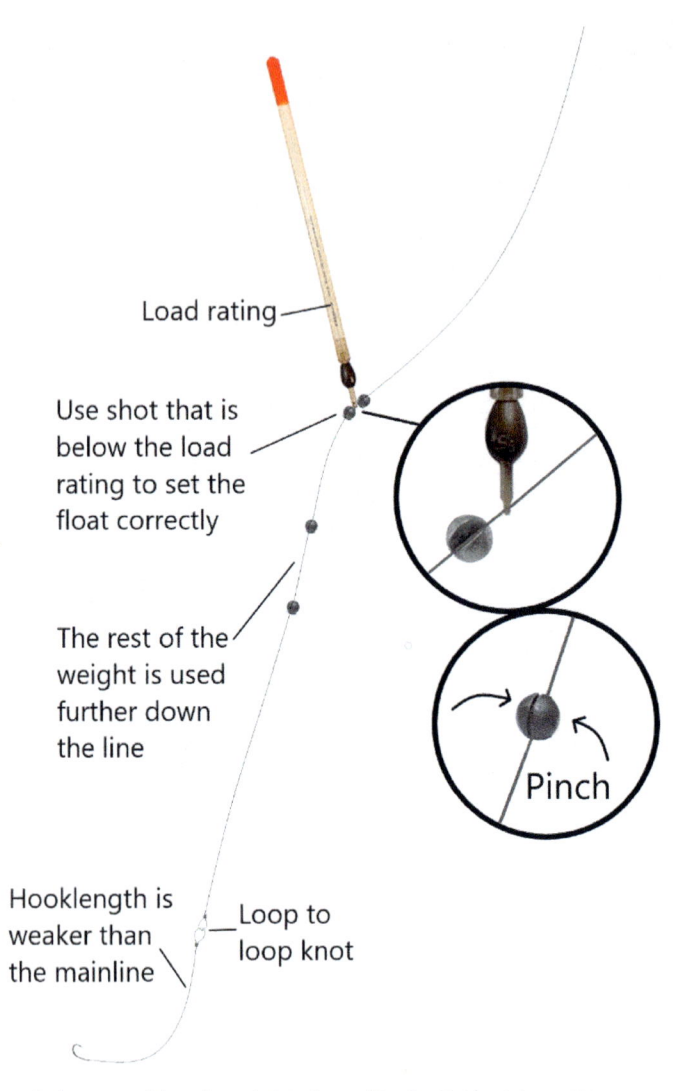

Loop to loop knot

Most of the rated load weight (in split shot) that is written on the side of the float body, is then pinched either side of it and then more shot is added down the line to make up the total rated load weight of the float or desired tip position.

How to attach a float using float rubbers

The pole float, avon float and the stick float are attached to the mainline by threading float rubbers onto the line.

Float rubbers should be just a little bit smaller than the section of float that it is going on to, this ensures that it has a secure fitment. You do not want them too tight, as you may need to adjust the position of the float during the session or when plumbing the depth.

You need a float rubber on the tip of the float, a float rubber just below the body of the float and you need one at the end of the stem (this sits half on the stem and half on the line to help avoid snagging).

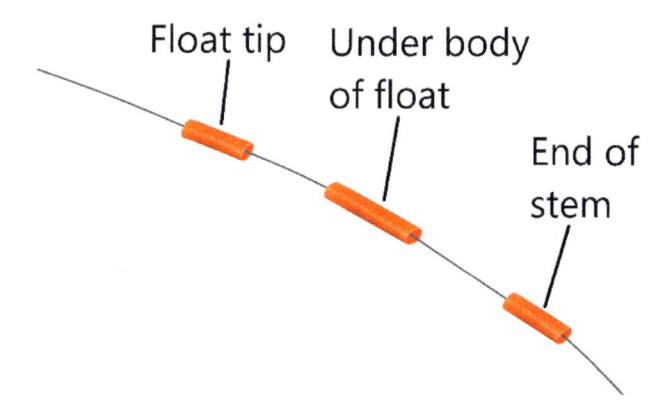

These rubbers once on the line, are then fitted onto the float in order.

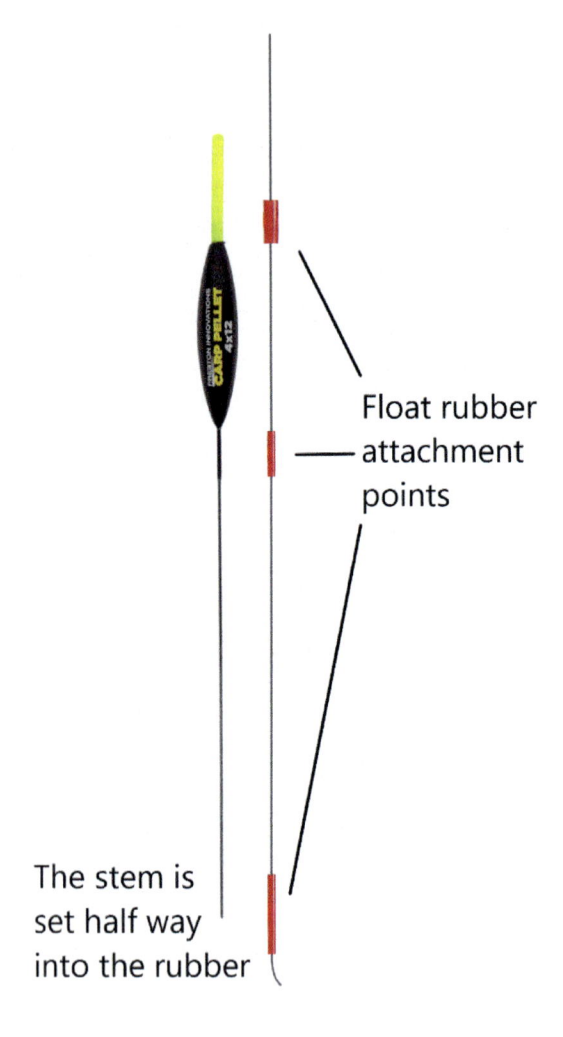

Float rubber attachment points

The stem is set half way into the rubber

Top Tip! With pole floats it is worthwhile very lightly lubricating the rubbers with water to make it easier to fit.

Float tip rubber

First fit the rubber to the tip by sliding it carefully over the tip of the float, pushing it from the tip down to the top of the body.

Middle (under body) rubber

The middle rubber is then pushed up the stem end of the float all the way until it is under the body or halfway.

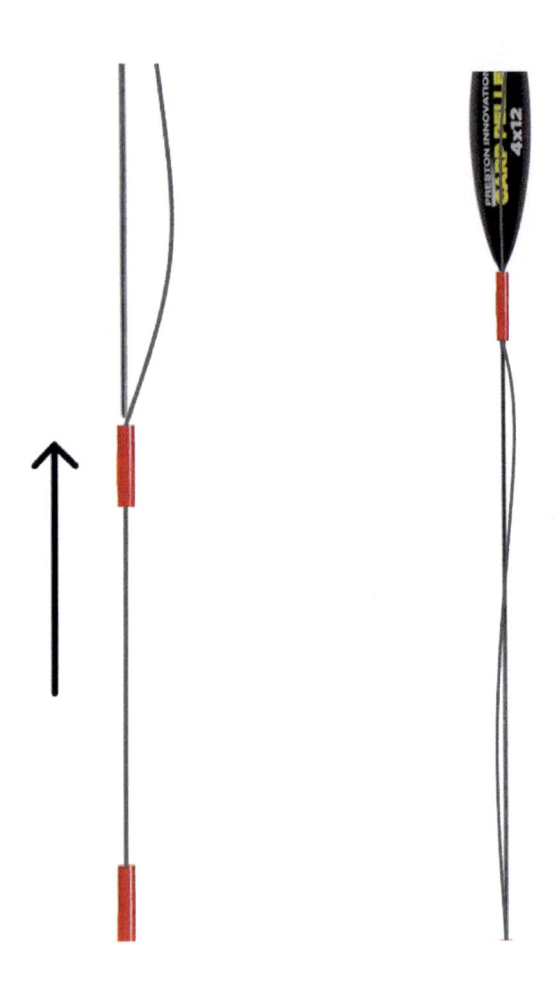

Bottom (end of stem) rubber

Then the bottom of the stem, the lowest one, is fitted half on the stem and half on the line. This is done so that the stem doesn't catch on anything or become a collection point for loose weeds etc.

As with attaching other floats, once it is on the line, you will need to tie a figure of 8 loop knot so that you can attach the hooklength. The hooklength is then attached to the mainline loop using a loop-to-loop knot.

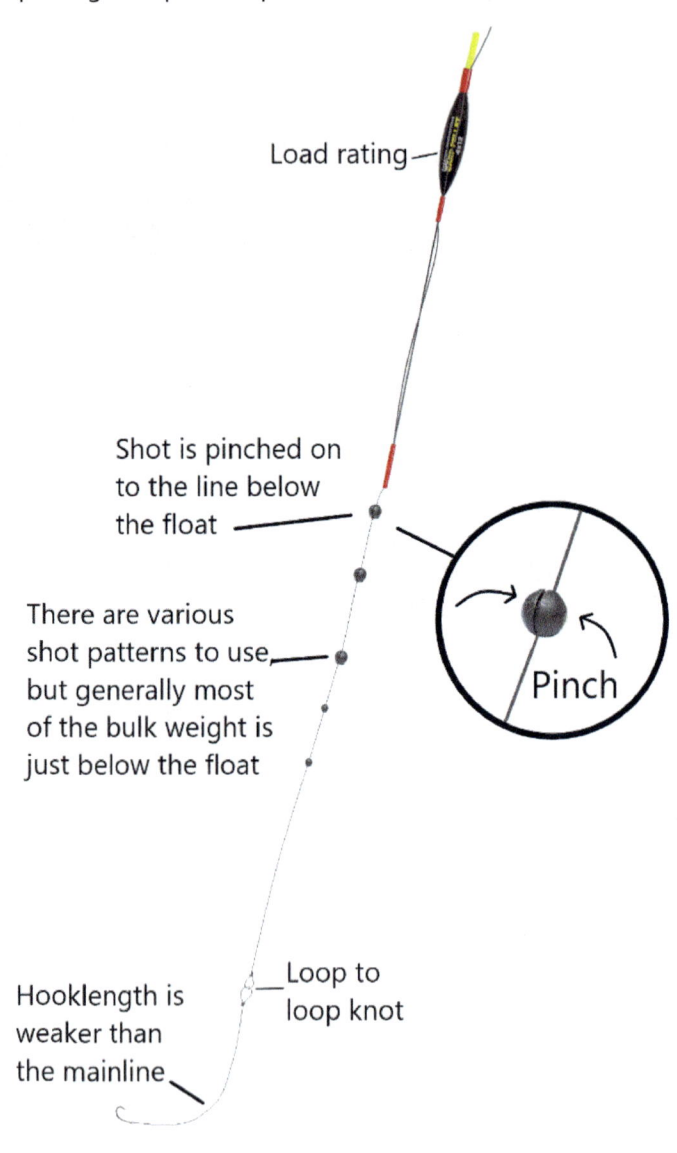

Load rating

Shot is pinched on to the line below the float

There are various shot patterns to use, but generally most of the bulk weight is just below the float

Pinch

Hooklength is weaker than the mainline

Loop to loop knot

What is plumbing the depth?

Plumbing the depth is the method in which you set a float's position in a way that allows you to have your hook bait fishing at the bottom of the water. This also tells you how deep the water is in the spot you are fishing, so is a very handy method to use to work out how the depth can change around your swim. You can use a plummet or large split shot on the hook apply this method.

A plummet

The plummet is used with the hook that is attached to your rig. Thread the hook through the eye of the plummet and then carefully pull it down to the bottom and hook it into the cork pad.

How do you plumb the depth?

The float rig is setup with the float attached to the line, this is either done by a threading it through the eye and adding split shot either side when using a waggler float (enough weight to allow it to sit correctly) or float rubbers if using a stick float or avon float. Worthwhile to find a float rig to use in the following sections as an idea on how to set them up. When setting the depth close in, you can swing it out using an underarm technique. Trapping the line as you would do normally when casting, instead of going over head, simply swing it out with a pendulum type momentum with a flicking action towards the end of the movement. If you need to go a little further, then standard overhead cast will work.

Plumbing the depth

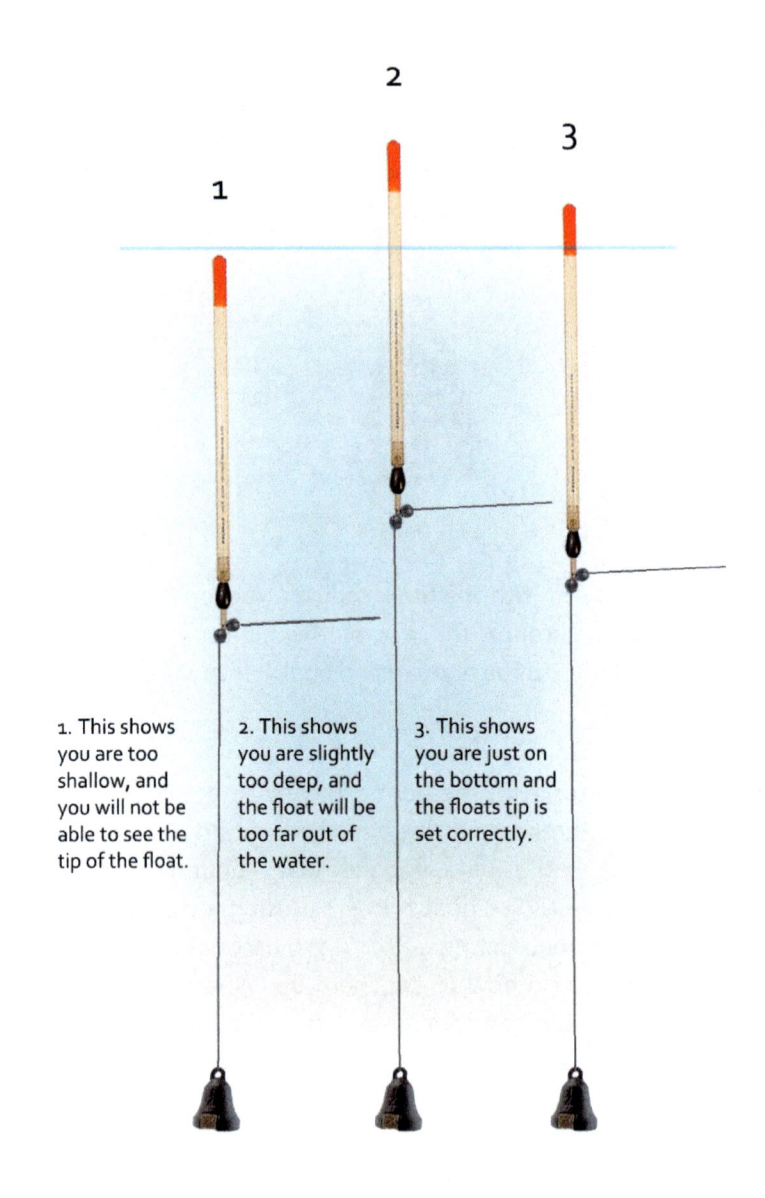

1. This shows you are too shallow, and you will not be able to see the tip of the float.

2. This shows you are slightly too deep, and the float will be too far out of the water.

3. This shows you are just on the bottom and the floats tip is set correctly.

What is a bite?

A bite is basically an indication that a fish is either attempting to eat your hookbait, or has eaten it. Sometimes an indication of the float dipping can also be fish knocking the rig, as it is suspended in the water column. Learning the difference takes time and experience, but there a a few ways to make sure you strike at the right time.

How to detect a bite when using a float

There are many ways to detect how a fish is biting, and you need to distinguish line bites and actual bites on the float. When fish are hitting the line, the float may knock and twitch. When a fish is mouthing at the bait, the float might dip.

Do not strike the float until you see the float disappear under the water. You can then be confident that the fish has been hooked and is swimming off with the bait. This doesn't happen all the time however, often bites that can be struck into, are missed. This is because the float has only very slightly been pulled downwards as the fish has mouthed the bait and released it, or fish like carp suck it in and then spit it back out. Learning the difference takes time, you will miss a lot of bites, but as long as you learn from it you will increase your catch rate.

A Simple Waggler rig

This is a simple waggler rig that will catch fish from stillwaters, canals and rivers. It is a basic float rig that every angler should know how to make.

1. A standard crystal waggler float, lock the float into position using two split shot, around 80% of the total rated weight. (Check load rating for recommended shot)

2. The strength of line will need to match the species of fish that you intend to or most likely catch. For the smaller species, its best to use mainline between 2lb-4lb, and for larger species use 4-6lb.

3. Place some smaller shot around half-way, between the float and the hook-length connection (small shot such as No 6 or No8 are a good starting point).

4. Place another two or three No8 shot equally spaced between the last shot and the hook. This allows the rig to fall through the water column.

5. Your hook length line needs to be a little weaker breaking strain than your mainline. Sometimes it is easier to use pre-tied hook lengths and attach them with a loop to loop knot.

6. If you want to target smaller silver fish such as Roach, Rudd or Bream then it would be best to have a hook size of around size 20-16 when fishing maggots. If you are using worms, corn or bread then hook size would be size 18-16.

Overdepth Waggler rig

The overdepth waggler rig is based on the simple waggler rig but the bait is laying flat on the bottom. You will need to plumb the depth on this rig, and aim to set the rig 4-6in overdepth so that the bait settles on the bottom

1. The float is locked onto the line using most of shot either side of the float. You want the tip to just be breaking through the surface.

2. The strength of line will need to match the species of fish you are targeting or mostliekly to catch.
For the smaller species, its best to use between 2lb-4lb, and for larger species use between 4-6lb.

3. Next place a few much smaller dropper shot just below halfway (small shot such as No 6 or No8 are a good starting point).

4. Further from this, inbetween the mid shot and the hook length connection, place another two or three No8 shot equally spaced between the last shot and the hook.
This will allow the bait to fall slowly through the water when it lands from casting, the bait falls gently down to the bottom.

5. Your hook length line needs to be a little weaker breaking strain than your mainline. So if you get snagged or the line breaks, it will only break here and not the whole rig.

6. If you want to target smaller silver fish such as Roach, Rudd or Bream then it would be best to have a hook size of around size 20-16 when fishing maggots. If using worms, corn or bread then use hook size 18-16. Aim to present your baited hook on the bottom between 4-6in overdepth.

Simple stick float trotting rig

Stick float fishing on a still water or trotting down a river can produce some excellent results. This rig can be used for most small silver fish to the big greedy Chub.

Feed and cast slightly downstream, and keeping the bail-arm open, pay out line to achieve a smooth trot, strike by trapping your finger on the spool.

1. Choose a stick float that has a highly visible domed top to help see the float at a long distance. You can work out the float size by the amount of depth you have, so for every 1ft of water you would want 1x No4 shot.

2. Float rubbers attach the float to the line, the lowest one needs to be over the end of the stem, this is to avoid snagging on anything that is floating in the water.

3. Shot can be used as a bulk well down the line, with a single smaller dropper shot below. In shallow swims the lack of depth means there's little time for the fish to see the bait falling. In deeper water you can adopt a spread of shot known as the shirt button-style pattern (as shown). Use smaller No6 shot to achieve a more natural fall of the bait.

4. For Chub, a 4lb-5lb mainline and a low-diameter hook length of a slightly lesser breaking strain are advised. As for hooks, size 16 or 14 would be ok. For smaller silver fish, a 2-3lb mainline and a low-diameter hook length of a slightly lesser breaking strain. Hook sizes from 18-20 would be ideal.

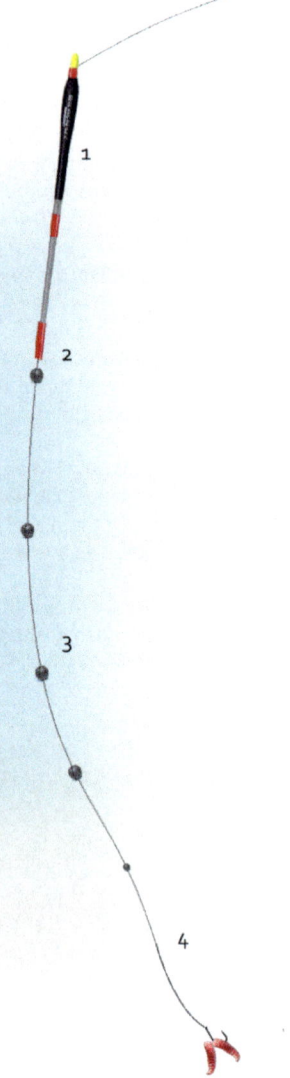

River stick float trotting rig

Trotting a river is an active method that involves flicking your rig out, paying out line from the reel, mending the line to make sure the float travels along the right line, and occasionally holding back the float to make the bait flutter off the bottom.

1. The best type of float to use when fishing slow-paced rivers and streams is a plastic, cane or carbon stemmed stick float as these are nice and light.

2. Float rubbers attach the float to the line, the lowest one needs to be over the end of the stem, this is to avoid snagging on anything that is floating in the water.

3. Once you have found the correct depth, mark it using a single No8 shot directly underneath the float.

4. The shot needs to be equally spaced down the line, but the majority of the weight needs to be positioned in the top two-thirds of the rig. Here pairs of shot have been used, equally spaced down the line. Pairs of No8 or No6 shot are ideal.

5. Choose a light floating mainline, around 2-3lb would be ideal for this rig. The floating line lifts off the water easily, therefore you can mend your line to keep control of the float really easily, plus you'll be able to strike fast bites easier too.

6. The last two shot should be set singularly to produce a slow and natural fall of the hook bait through the last foot or so of water. No8 shot are ideal for this.

7. The hook needs to suit the bait that you are fishing with, although a size 16 would be an ideal starting point that will help hook most fish.

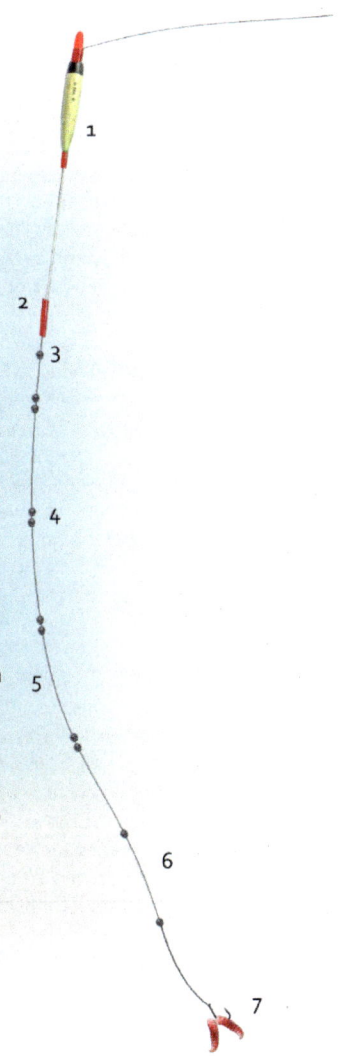

Avon style float rig

When you are fishing the fast and shallow swims, often shadowed by willow trees, aiming to catch the big chub or barbel, it is a very formidable task. With the faster pace of water, you need to use a heavy Avon-style float taking several AAA shot to not only give you great control of the rig but to also get the bait down to the bottom quickly.

1. Float size - With the river running at full pace, your float won't be in the swim for that long because it will soon trot out of the peg. So, to get the bait to the bottom at the top of the swim, pick a large sized avon float (large stick float with a big upper body and tip) taking around 4-5 AAA shot. This will let the float cock immediately and begin fishing because a bite can often come right at the head of the swim.

2. Lines and hooks also need to be strong, around 5-6lb and upward (if snaggy areas, then use 8lb).

3. The Bulk shot - This means a shotting pattern made up of all the float's weight grouped into a bulk just above the hook link. Typically, this will be made up of large BB or AAA shot, and in shallow swims this method can get you more bites.

4. Not only are the Chub and Barbel hard fighting fish, but they also love going straight to the snags. The riverbed may also be uneven, with lots of rocks. Naturally, a hooked fish will do its best to cut you off by rubbing the line against these snags. It makes sense then, to use heavy tackle with a hook link of around 0.16mm or 0.18mm and a strong size 14 or 12 hook for fishing big baits.

Chubber (Loafer) float rig

The short, fat, and dumpy chubber float (Also known as a loafer) is perfect for fishing shallow and fast rivers or trotting on streams. It has a lot of buoyancy and can carry a lot of shot. This is perfect for fast and shallow swims, as they need a lot of lead down the line to ensure that the bait is pushed down to the bottom right where the fish are.

1. Your mainline ideally should be a floating variety and has a breaking strain that matches the fish that you are likely to catch. A 3lb line will be adequate for most situations, but you may need to step up to 5 or even 6lb if there are lots of big barbel present.

2. The chubber float can to be attached to the mainline using three rubbers – one just under the sight tip, one in the middle and one at the base of the float as you would a pole or stick float. Alternatively, you can just use one float rubber on the tip and thread the line through the float connector at the bottom.

3. To shot a chubber float – you can either use a string of large shot (BBs, AAs or even SSGs) placed around 1ft from the hook, or you can use an olivette (a tapered weight that line passes through internally). This creates a much smaller and neater bulk of weight.

4. With this rig being mainly used in fast water, the fish don't have that much time to see the hook length, so you can tie it straight through to your hook. You still need to match the hook size to the size of the bait you are using.

General maggot pole rig

This general maggot pole float rig can be used in most situations, perfectly suited to most lakes and still waters. This can work very well in depths from 3ft to 7ft.

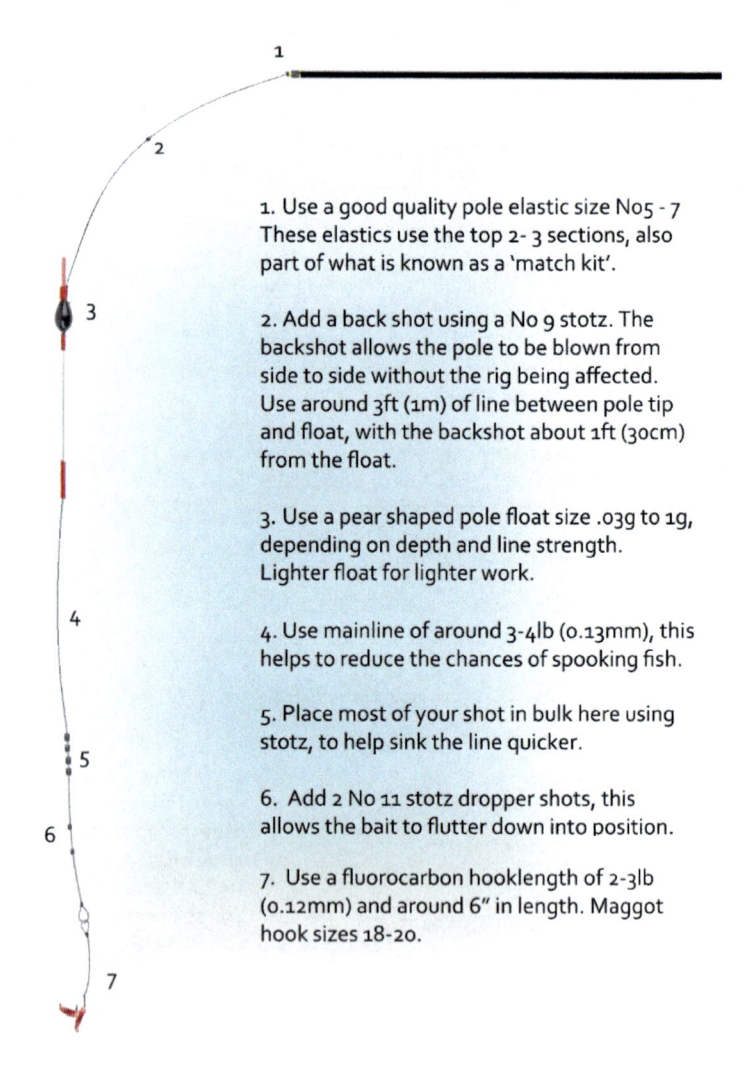

1. Use a good quality pole elastic size No5 - 7 These elastics use the top 2- 3 sections, also part of what is known as a 'match kit'.

2. Add a back shot using a No 9 stotz. The backshot allows the pole to be blown from side to side without the rig being affected. Use around 3ft (1m) of line between pole tip and float, with the backshot about 1ft (30cm) from the float.

3. Use a pear shaped pole float size .03g to 1g, depending on depth and line strength. Lighter float for lighter work.

4. Use mainline of around 3-4lb (0.13mm), this helps to reduce the chances of spooking fish.

5. Place most of your shot in bulk here using stotz, to help sink the line quicker.

6. Add 2 No 11 stotz dropper shots, this allows the bait to flutter down into position.

7. Use a fluorocarbon hooklength of 2-3lb (0.12mm) and around 6" in length. Maggot hook sizes 18-20.

Pole float - Winter silver fish rig

This winter silver fish rig can be used in most situations during the colder months and is well suited to most lakes and still waters. This rig works well in depths from 2ft - 5ft.

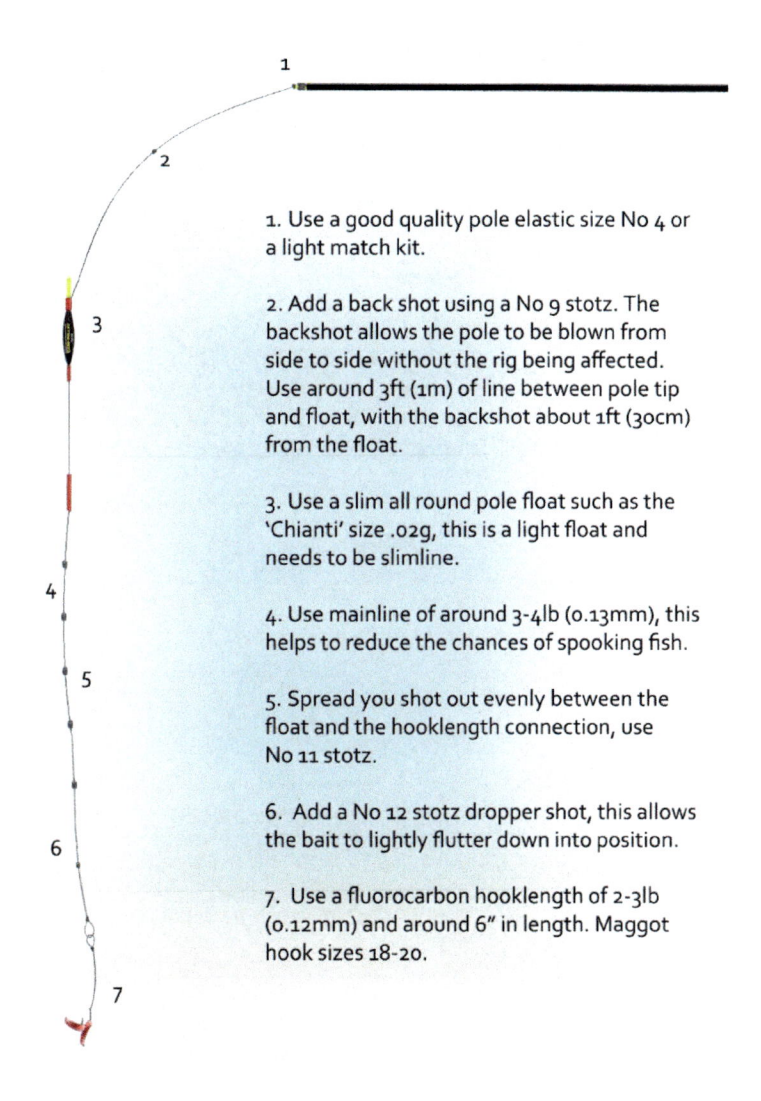

1. Use a good quality pole elastic size No 4 or a light match kit.

2. Add a back shot using a No 9 stotz. The backshot allows the pole to be blown from side to side without the rig being affected. Use around 3ft (1m) of line between pole tip and float, with the backshot about 1ft (30cm) from the float.

3. Use a slim all round pole float such as the 'Chianti' size .02g, this is a light float and needs to be slimline.

4. Use mainline of around 3-4lb (0.13mm), this helps to reduce the chances of spooking fish.

5. Spread you shot out evenly between the float and the hooklength connection, use No 11 stotz.

6. Add a No 12 stotz dropper shot, this allows the bait to lightly flutter down into position.

7. Use a fluorocarbon hooklength of 2-3lb (0.12mm) and around 6" in length. Maggot hook sizes 18-20.

Feeder Fishing

A guide to the basic feeder fishing techniques

Simple free running feeder rig

This simple yet very effective free running feeder fishing rig is perfect for catching a fish from the river or most still waters. To use this for bigger fish such as Chub, Barbel or Carp, use a bigger sized hook and feeder. For smaller fish, use a small feeder with a small hook. It's easy to make and can be used in deep sluggish rivers to fairly shallow and swift flowing rivers, to deep lakes, to close in the margins.

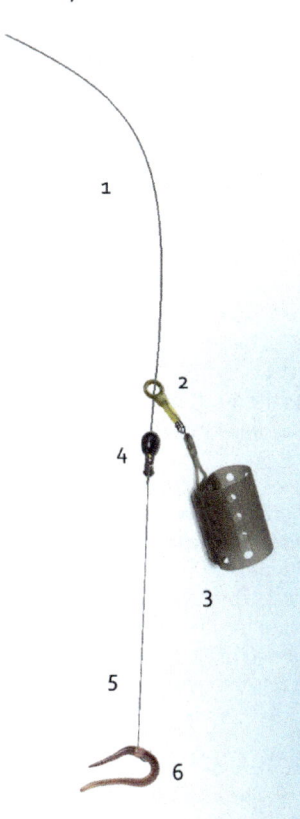

1. Use mainline from 6lb - 8lb when fishing stillwaters or when light feeder fishing on rivers for Chub. Use 10lb - 12lb when using this rig for heavier feeder fishing on rivers or for larger species like Carp.

2. Using a run ring quick change adapter (or similar) this will help you to swap to different feeders, saving time on the bank.

3. For stillwaters use a meduim sized feeder 12g - 30g for casting distances upto 30m, use 30g - 45g to cast upto 50m. Use a feeder upto 50g - 70g for casting 70m or more. For rivers use feeders 30g upwards to just hold bottom, if faster flow use heavier feeder. A fishmeal based goundbait is always a good starting point.

4. Use a quick change bead to attach the hooklength, this also acts as a buffer bead for the run ring.

5. Use a fluorocarbon hooklength of around 5lb - 8lb dependant of target species. From 6" to 18" in length on stillwaters, and upto 3ft depending on flow for rivers.

6. Hook sizes depend on species, size 14 - 16 when using maggots, worms or sweetcorn. It is also worth using hair rigs for pellets and other baits, size 10 - 14 hooks can be used.

Method feeder rig

Method feeder fishing presents a hook bait that is moulded within groundbait or pellets. This method feeder rig is ideal for beginners, easy to set up and easy to use. Method feeders come with moulds to help set the groundbait onto the frame of the feeder, but this can also still be done by hand.

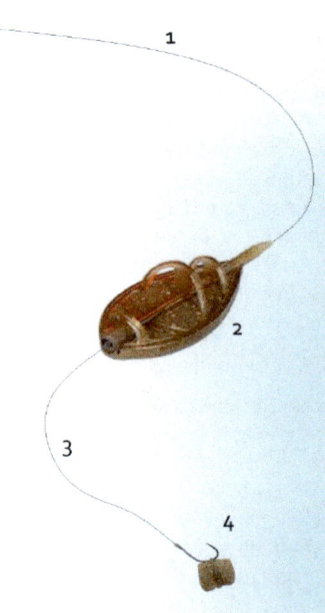

1. Use a mainline of around 8lb, as this will help when casting as the weight of the groundbait/pellets as well as the feeder can add a fair amount of weight to the line (this doesn't include the fish on the end of it). Up the strength if targeting bigger species.

2. Use a feeder with around 20g to 30g, you can also use a hybrid feeder in place of the method. There are so many method feeder specific groundbaits to choose from, but you can also use soaked pellets. Make sure your mix is not too wet or too dry. Thread the mainline through the attachment tube, then through the feeder and tie it onto the connector.

3. Use a hooklength that is weaker than the mainline. The hooklength can be from 4" to 6" and needs to be supple. If you are targeting large carp, then use a braided line (if allowed). This is connected to the feeder by the quick-change connector supplied with the feeder. You can also use a quick-change bead or swivel.

4. Use a size 12 to 16 hook, depending on the bait being used. If you are using pellets on the feeder, then use a hooklength with a pellet band. If using sweetcorn or meat, then use a quickstop.
There are so many premade hooklengths to buy for method feeder rigs. You can also use boilies, wafters as these tend to be brightly coloured and highly attractive. Try not to use live bait as they tend to either break up the moulding or are crushed by it.

Maggot feeder rig

This really easy to use maggot feeder rig can be used anywhere. It is perfect for most rivers or stillwaters. To use this for larger venues, use a bigger sized maggot feeder. It's really simple to make and can be used on fast rivers to small shallow streams, to deep lakes, to close in the margins. It all depends on how far you need to cast and how much bait you wish to dispense.

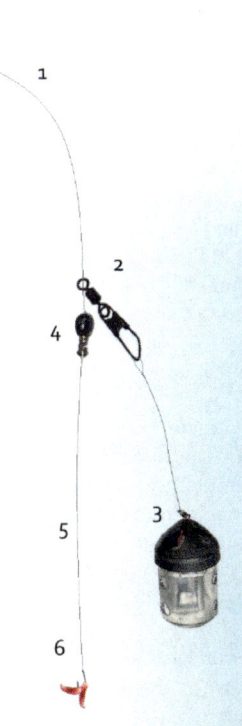

1. Use mainline from 5lb - 8lb when fishing stillwaters or when light feeder fishing on rivers for Chub. Use 8lb - 10lb when using this rig for fishing on rivers or for larger species like Carp.

2. Use a swivel snap link connector (or similar) as this will help you to swap to different sizes of feeders. Connect the feeder with a 6"- 10" link made up of 8lb line. Tie it to the feeder and then make a loop knot at the end to attach it to the connector.

3. For Stillwater, use a small or medium sized maggot feeder. These feeders range in both size and weight (they can be same weight but a different size). Similar to the other feeders, the weights have similar casting ranges. 10g - 30g for casting distances up to 30m, use 30g - 50g to cast up to 50m. Maggots, castors, hemp, 2mm pellets and chopped worm are a few of the baits to use.

4. Use a quick-change bead (or similar) to attach the hooklength, this also acts as a buffer bead for the swivel connector.

5. Use a fluorocarbon hooklength of around 3lb - 8lb dependant of target species. From 6" to 12" in length on stillwaters, and up to 3ft depending on flow for rivers.

6. Hook sizes depend on species, use hook sizes of 14 - 16 when using live baits such as maggots, castors, or worms.

Helicopter feeder rig

This type of feeder rig is virtually tangle-free, and very simple to set up. It is a very effective way to catch fish on slow-flowing rivers and lakes, and a great way to present hookbait. You can use many different feeders with this, so the bait options are plentiful to choose from.

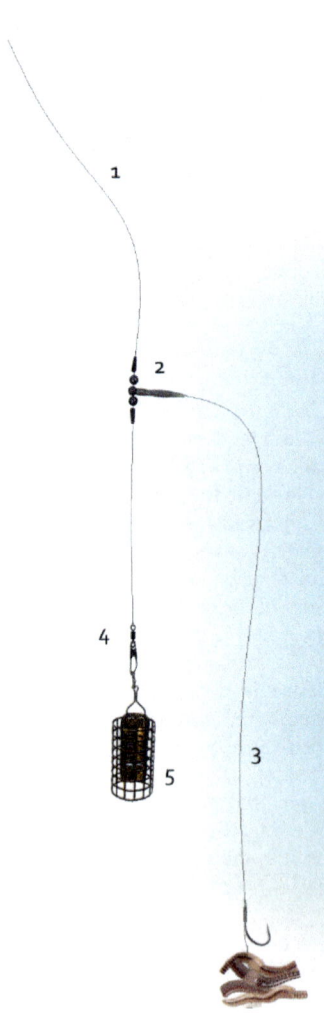

1. Use mainline from 6lb - 12lb when fishing stillwaters depending on target species or when light feeder fishing on rivers for Chub, use 6lb - 8lb.

2. Use a connector specifically designed for the helicopter style rig, as these are very quick to use. This essentially is a swivel connector in the middle, two buffer beads either side and two float stops either side of them. But you can also use a swivel and two large float stops either side if fishing a light setup just as well. The whole point of this setup is to allow you to set the hook connection point to your desired position, and also to reduce tangles as the hooklength swivels around the feeder and slightly away from it.

3. You can use premade hooklengths, hair rigs or whatever suits your target species and bait being used. This setup can be used for all types of bait, ranging from maggots to boilies. Ideally use fluorocarbon, of around 8" - 12" + in length on stillwaters and up to 2ft depending on flow when using it on rivers.

4. Tie a swivel connector to the end of the line 4" 6" from hooklength point, this allows you to quickly connect any feeder to suit your style of fishing, should that change throughout a session.

5. As with most feeder rigs, choose a feeder that suits both application and distance. This rig is popular with Tench anglers, using chopped worm, worm soil and a little fishmeal based groundbait as feed with a juicy worm chopped up on the hook (using a quickstop).

213

Ledger Fishing

A guide to basic ledgering techniques

Simple free running rig

This simple free running ledger fishing rig is perfect for catching all sorts of fish from the river or most stillwaters. It's easy to make and can be used in deep weir pools to fairly shallow and swift flowing rivers, to various lakes, to close up in the margins. This can be used with a various amounts of leads, any shape or weight.

1. Use mainline from 6lb - 8lb when on stillwaters or when light ledger fishing on rivers for Chub. Use 10lb - 12lb when using this rig for heavier flow on rivers or at long range for larger species like Carp.

2. Using a run ring quick change adapter (or similar) this will help you to swap to different leads or change over to a feeder.

3. The casting weights are similar to feeders, but with a slight difference when choosing which one to use. Lead weights come in many shapes and sizes, so choosing the right one is critical. Flat leads (and gripper) are used to ensure the rig rests easier on the surface, more so when it is a gradient like the edge of an island. Rounder leads (like the Arlesey bomb) are used on hard surfaces or when you want the rig to have a roll to it. Also be sure of the surface your rig is sitting on, as if it is silt based, you wouldn't want to use a heavy pointed lead, or it would get stuck or use a round lead on an incline as it would roll away.

4. Use a quick-change bead to attach the hooklength, this also acts as a buffer bead for the run ring.

5. Use a fluorocarbon hooklength of around 5lb - 8lb dependant of target species. From 6" to 18" in length on stillwaters, and up to 3ft depending on flow for rivers. If Carp fishing, use a short braided hooklink (if allowed) of around 4" - 6".

6. Hook sizes depend on species, size 14 - 16 when using maggots, worms, or sweetcorn. It is also worth using hair rigs for pellets and other baits, size 10 - 14 hooks can be used.

The Link ledger rig

This link ledger rig is perfect for the roving angler, easy to setup and very light to carry around finding swims to fish in whilst walking along the river. This rig is also useful for small lakes, ponds, and streams. Really ideal for catching Chub, Dace, Roach, Rudd, and Perch. You can use any bait you want, and loose feed by hand as and when needed to get the fish feeding.

1. Use mainline from 6lb to 8lb when on rivers and small stillwaters, make sure it is a good high quality abrasion resistant line.

2. Use a swivel to allow the shot to run up and down the line freely.

3. Tie a 4" length of line on to the swivel, pinch on 3 to 4 SSG shot. The shot can be taken off or more added depending on flow, you want enough to just allow the rig to roll with the current very slightly. You can also use this with a slight bolt effect by adding extra to just hold bottom.

4. Use a quick-change bead to allow the hooklengths to be changed over quickly, but it also acts as a buffer bead for the swivel.

5. Use a hooklength of 6"- 24" depending on the flow. Use 5lb-7lb fluorocarbon.

6. If you are using live baits such as maggot, castor, or small worms then use a hook size of 14-16. If you are using a big lobworm, then use a hook 8 - 12 depending on species (Chub have huge mouths so a size 8 is good). If you are using bread flake, then use a hook that fits the size of flake (hook sizes 6 - 12 ideally).

Basic Carp fishing pop-up rig

This Carp fishing rig is perfect for catching not just Carp, but all sorts of fish from most stillwaters and rivers. It's easy to make and can be used with various pop-up boilies and wafters, bottom baits and much more.

1. Use mainline from 12lb to 15lb when on stillwaters or on rivers, make sure it is a good quality line.

2. Using a lead clip, thread mainline through the sleeve, then through the clip and tie to the swivel. moisten the clip before fitting the sleeve in place. It is important not to push it on to tight, as it is designed to shake off the lead if the fish is snagged when playing it.

3. The casting weights are similar to feeders, but with a slight difference when choosing which one to use. Lead weights come in many shapes and sizes, so choosing the right one is critical. You need to be sure of the lake/river bed that the rig is sitting on, if it is silt based, you wouldn't want to use a heavy pointed lead, or it would get stuck. If you use a pointed lead on an incline it would roll away. Rounder, and more pointed leads are used on hard surfaces, but also good for longer range fishing.

4. Use an anti-tangle sleeve on your hooklink to keep the swivel covered and give a stiffer attachment point to prevent tangles.

5. Use a braided hooklength (if allowed) from 18lb to 25lb dependant of target species. From 4" to 6" in length (use a coated braid if using for pop-ups or wafters).

6. Place some tungsten putty or a meduim sized shot 1" from the hook if using pop-ups. If using coated braid, strip away 5mm-8mm before adding to give it flexiblilty.

7. Hook sizes depend on the bait, size 2 - 8 can be used when fishing with boilies or large pellets for Carp (8 - 12 for other species). The hook size is also dependant on weather and time of year, smaller more discreet hooks are an advantage in winter.

The Snowman rig

This Carp fishing rig is perfect for catching not just Carp, but all sorts of fish from most stillwaters and rivers. It's easy to make and can be used with various pop-up boilies and wafters, bottom baits and much more.

1. Use mainline from 12lb to 15lb when on stillwaters or on rivers, make sure it is a good quality line.

2. Use a strong swivel connector or large rung ring to attach the lead to. Thread on a buffer bead or large stop.

3. This particluar rig, you want to attach a 3oz lead, but as with the other ledger rigs, the casting weights are to be considered. Also remember that lead weights come in many shapes and sizes, so choosing the right one is critical. You need to be sure of the lake/river bed that the rig is sitting on, if it is silt based, you wouldn't want to use a heavy pointed lead, or it would get stuck. If you use a pointed lead on an incline it would roll away. Rounder, and more pointed leads are used on hard surfaces, but are also good for longer range fishing.

4. Use a large quick change swivel connector, also fit an anti-tangle sleeve on your hooklink to keep the swivel covered and give a stiffer attachment point to prevent tangles.

5. Use a braided hooklength (if allowed) from 18lb to 25lb dependant of target species and around 8" in length.

6. Hook sizes depend on the bait, size 2 - 8 can be used when fishing with boilies or large pellets for Carp (8 - 12 for other species). The hook size is also dependant on weather and time of year, smaller more discreet hooks are an advantage in winter.

7. Using a large 14mm - 18mm bottom bait boilie and a 10mm - 12mm pop-up boilie, tie a knotless knot to your hook, you want around a 2" hair rig.

218

Essential Links

Links to organisations and affiliates to AMHI

Angling organisations and affiliate links

Licensing bodies (England & Wales)

www.gov.uk/government/organisations/environment-agency

Lead bodies for angling (England & Wales)

www.anglingtrust.net

The Angling and Mental Health Initiative (AMHI) and this book have been supported by:

The Angling Trust is the united national representative body for all angling in England and Wales. It is united in collaborative relationships with Fish Legal, a separate membership association that uses the law to protect fish stocks and the rights of its members throughout the UK.

Environment Agency

The Environment Agency reinvests money from fishing license sales to provide more opportunities to go fishing and make improvements to angling habitats and infrastructure.

SPORT ENGLAND

Sports England is committed to helping people and communities across the country to create sporting habits for life. It funds the Angling Trust to strengthen the angling core market by supporting people to keep fishing, and to deliver an England talent pathway to competition.

The Let's Go Fishing! – The Angling and Mental Health Initiative

We would also like to take this opportunity to give thanks to the hard work and support that the Angling Trust have given this project. This has not only come in the form of funding but also giving support to the project and how to manage it. Using the platform for the Get Fishing scheme has had a huge impact on local communities and we are grateful and proud to be part of it and its success.

The 'Get Fishing' campaign is run by the Angling Trust to increase the number of people being introduced to angling across the country. Fishing events for everyone regardless of age, gender, fitness, or previous experience can be found by using the QR code above.

TOGETHER FUND

The Together Fund is a continuation of the Tackling Inequalities Fund that was set up in April 2020 as part of their support package to help the sport and physical activity sector through the coronavirus (Covid-19) crisis. Since its launch, TIF has enabled community groups to continue to exist and engage with their communities, supporting people to be engaged and active.

Acknowledgements

Special thanks to Bodle Angling for supporting the local development project as part of the Haywards Heath & District Angling Society (HHDAS) in Mid Sussex, their role in the projects and the Let's Go Fishing! Open Day events has been amazing and allowed the events to be really successful.

A huge thank you to the committee at Haywards Heath & District Angling Society (HHDAS) for all the hard work volunteering and coaching at the Let's Go Fishing! – Open Day events held on their venue. For allowing the use of the venue at Valebridge Mill Pond, a beautiful estate lake surrounded by a nature reserve with amazing landscapes and that is a key part of the AMHI. A big thank you to the HHDAS committee for their photos, advice and sharing their knowledge that helped with the book and its contents.

Printed in Great Britain
by Amazon